THE OTHER GUIDE TO SAN FRANCISCO

or 105
Things to Do After You've Taken a Cable Car to Fisherman's Wharf

THE OTHER GUIDE TO SAN FRANCISCO

or

105

Things to Do After You've Taken a Cable Car to Fisherman's Wharf

By Jay Hansen

Illustrated by Tim Boxell

Designed by Diane Hoyt-Goldsmith

Chronicle Books/San Francisco

To my father
a truly great and good man

Copyright © 1980 by Stephen Jay Hansen.
All rights reserved.
Printed in the United States of America.

Library of Congress Cataloging in Publication Data

Hansen, Jay.
    The other guide to San Francisco.

    1.   San Francisco—Description—Guide-books.
I.   Title.
F869.S33H36   917.94'61'045   79-24740
ISBN 0-87701-163-X

Composition by Hansen and Associates.

Book and cover design by Diane Hoyt-Goldsmith.

Chronicle Books
870 Market Street
San Francisco, CA 94102

Table of Contents

THE TEN MOST POPULAR THINGS TO DO

DON'T MISS

ONLY IN SAN FRANCISCO

FISHERMAN'S WHARF

CHINATOWN

NORTH BEACH

UNION STREET

DOWNTOWN

SPOT TOURS

SPARE PARTS

Thanks

For their help, support and friendship: Terri Adams, Freddie Avner, Alessandro Baccari, Lara Bell, Brian Brooks, Bob Brown, Cynthia Bowman, Cathy Boxell, Mark Carver, Paula Finn, Rory Flood, Ben Fong-Torres, Delores French, David Gest, Robert Goodhue, Herbie Herbert, the staff and management of the Hotel Henry, Jack Jensen, Susan King, Carly Lee, Bobby McGee, Pat Morrow, Susan Mullen, George Pillsbury, Terry Pimsleur, Rickie Prescott, the San Francisco Public Library, Patty Schneider, Dick Schuettge, Martha Sternberg, Bret Taylor, Queenie Taylor, Abraham Totah, Lyle Tuttle, and Susan Weisberg.

Special thanks to: My family, Mercedes Tondre, Mikey (Razor) Raskovsky, Dierdre Gentry, Diane Hoyt-Goldsmith, and Jane Vandenburgh; to Lee Abrams for getting me to San Francisco in the first place and to Lou Galliani for first turning me on to the City.

But most of all, my eternal gratitude to the three people who gave me the nerve to start this thing in the first place: My father, H Kenneth Hansen, my friend Tim Boxell, and my main inspiration, Myra Zylstra. In the words of Huckleberry Finn, ". . . if I'd a knowed what a trouble it was to make a book I wouldn't a tackled it and aint't agoing to no more."

Introduction

Let's face it: San Francisco needs another guidebook like it needs another hill.

What it could use is a break from the glut of guides that divide the City and your day into neat little components, fawn over buildings and stores and hold out the promise of the "perfect" day in San Francisco (sorry, but any city that can't clear 70° F in July is far from perfect).

What it could use is *The Other Guide to San Francisco (Or, 105 Things To Do After You've Taken a Cable Car To Fisherman's Wharf)*.

The idea is to allow you freedom of choice. Two things were uppermost in my mind as I wrote *The Other Guide*: 1) You know what you like to do. 2) If you know where to look to find what you like to do, it's a lot easier to do it. I show you where to find San Francisco: past, present, warts and all. I leave it to you to decide how to spend your time, so you can enjoy it at your pace and to your taste. That way you'll hopefully feel less like a tourist, stumbling from sight to sight, and more like a short-term resident, involved in the day-to-day life of the City. So get out and do it, bearing in mind a couple of things: Hours, prices and even places change. The information in the book is correct as of publication, but to be safe, call ahead to confirm your plans wherever possible.

Although the book is arranged numerically, you certainly don't have to read it sequentially. In fact, you might want to check out the last item first. Since you'll doubtless be doing a lot of eating out, you'll want to know where the best restaurants are. I polled fifty famous San Franciscans for their favorite turn-ons, for a list that runs the gamut of San Francisco's incredible edible experiences.

That's it. Thanks for buying my book. I hope you have as much fun using it as I did researching it.

TEN MOST POPULAR THINGS TO DO IN SAN FRANCISCO

1	Fisherman's Wharf
2	Cable Cars
3	Chinatown
4	Golden Gate Bridge
5	Alcatraz
6	Lombard Street
7	Union Street
8	Sausalito
9	Coit Tower
10	Golden Gate Park

1 Fisherman's Wharf

Hands down, the most popular attraction in San Francisco is Fisherman's Wharf. The once-musty wharf area has undergone a dramatic overhaul since the 1950s to become an All-American review of native attractions, shops and restaurants. You can visit wax, wine and sailing museums; take a helicopter tour or a deep-sea fishing excursion; be entertained by street musicians or enthralled by street artists; or simply shop and eat at one of the three outstanding restoration projects on the Wharf—Ghirardelli Square, The Cannery or Pier 39.

So what are you waiting for? Turn to page 100 for some ideas of what to do on the Wharf—if you need any. Also, check out number 22 to find out where you can peek in on the mysterious sourdough process, and number 11 for the inside scoop on a liquid legend that originated on Fisherman's Wharf.

2 Cable Cars

San Francisco's charming little cable cars have been climbing halfway to the stars for more than a century now. You haven't even begun to experience San Francisco until you've hopped one for an open-air tumble up and down San Francisco's fabled hills. Get going, and on the way enjoy the story of how San Francisco's cable cars came and continue to be.

The cable car was born in storybook fashion one cold, wet winter's evening back in 1869. It was on that night that a young Scotsman named Andrew Hallidie watched a team of horses, wagon in tow, struggle up one of San Francisco's steep hills. Just as they reached the top, one of the horses lost its footing, sending all four to the bottom of the hill in a bloody heap. Properly horrified, Hallidie resolved then and there that no horse would ever again suffer such a cruel fate. (Never mind that Hallidie had already designed a similar cable system for moving ore out of the mountains—this is *legend* that we're dealing with.)

The world, as it is wont to do, snickered at "Hallidie's Folly." But the Scotsman persevered, and at 5 AM on 1 August 1873 he piloted the world's first cable car on a five-block descent into history.

The public (to say nothing of the horses) immediately took to the idea of cable cars. Hills that had been consigned to goats and damn fools suddenly came under colonization. By 1906 eight cable car companies were successfully operating some six hundred cars over 110 miles of track. (In comparison, the three remaining lines today operate thirty-nine cars over seventeen miles of track.) San Francisco had, if not exactly rapid transit, at least a steady, sure-footed system.

The San Francisco cable car peaked, however, with the Great Earthquake and Fire of 1906. Most of the cars and much of the track were wiped out. A few of the lines were subsequently converted to electric trolley systems, while others disappeared altogether as San Francisco got itself deeper and deeper into the twentieth century. By the 1950s only a few lines remained, and the smart money was betting against their survival.

Enter the good people of San Francisco, who in 1955 amended the city charter to provide for the "maintenance and perpetuation" of the cable car. (Only a majority vote by the public can ever overturn this charter amendment, and that isn't very likely.) In 1964, the U.S. government seconded the motion by declaring San Francisco's cable cars a National Historic Landmark. And so they continue to track on, just as Andrew Hallidie envisioned over a century ago.

CABLE CAR FACTS

Average yearly passenger load (all three cable car lines): 13 million

Weight of each cable car: 6 tons

Speed: 9 miles per hour (never faster, never slower)

Steepest grade: Hyde Street, between Bay and Francisco Streets near Fisherman's Wharf, has a 21.3 percent grade (which means it rises about one foot vertically for every five feet horizontally)

Number of "Danger" signs on each cable car:

12 (California line)

6 (Powell Street lines)

In spite of those warnings, San Francisco quietly pays out a number of damage suits every year, averaging $100,000, but running as high as $900,000.

Most famous settlement: In 1964, a Hyde Street cable car slipped its brakes and plummeted down Hyde Street into a power pole. One of the passengers, 24-year-old Gloria Sykes, later sued the City for $500,000 in damages, claiming that the accident had turned her into a nymphomaniac, with an intense need for "the vibrations of the (male) body." Her condition, her lawyers argued, could be set off by the mere meeting of eyes on the street, resulting in literally hundreds of sexual liaisons. The judge sympathized, to a point, and Gloria Sykes was awarded $35,000 by the City of San Francisco to help ease her shame.

Where they go: *The #61 California Street Line* runs east and west along a 17-block stretch of California Street. It starts at the Embarcadero Center, cuts through the Financial District, passes through Chinatown, goes over Nob Hill and crosses trendy Polk Street before it reverses itself at Van Ness and California Streets.

The #59 Powell-Mason and *#60 Powell-Hyde Street Lines* share the same track from the busy downtown Powell Street turnaround until just after they cross Nob Hill. They go their own separate ways to Fisherman's Wharf from there.

The #60 Powell-Hyde Street Line trips up Russian Hill, passes Lombard Street (The World's Crookedest) and plunges into Fisherman's Wharf near Ghirardelli Square and The Cannery.

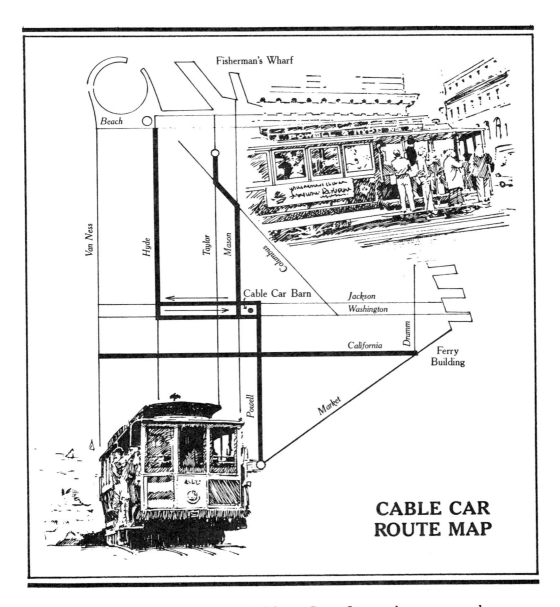

Fisherman's Wharf

Beach

Van Ness

Hyde

Taylor

Mason

Columbus

Cable Car Barn

Jackson

Washington

California

Drumm

Ferry Building

Powell

Market

CABLE CAR ROUTE MAP

The #59 Powell-Mason Street Line makes a more sedate crossing of Russian Hill, passes through North Beach and ends up at a nondescript corner in Fisherman's Wharf near Pier 39.
The best ride: For raw thrills and pure value, it's the #60 Powell-Hyde Street Line, hands down.

How they work: Imagine a skier being hauled up a hill on a rope tow. Well, the cable car is like that skier, clinging tenaciously to the cable (which runs at a constant 9 mph just below the surface of the street) by means of the "grip," a vertical lever that the gripman fusses over. The heavier the load or steeper the hill, the tighter the grip on the cable. And that's it—just simple friction. No rancid fumes and no fancy combustion systems. Isn't it nice to ride on something that you can understand?

Hours of operation:

#61 California Street Line:

Mon.-Fri. 6 a.m.-11 p.m.; Sat., Sun. and holidays 7:15 a.m. 11 p.m.

#59 Powell-Mason Street Line and *#60 Powell-Hyde Street Line:*

Mon.-Sat. 6 a.m.-1 a.m.; Sundays and holidays 6:30-1 a.m.

3 CHINATOWN

It's not all that dark and unfathomable, just a little confusing. So much so, in fact, that the first time through Chinatown the best you can hope for is to make it out before your senses overload. Chinatown is the one part of San Francisco where it's helpful to have a good guide—which, fortunately, you do, right here in your hands. Turn to page 110 for a brief history of Chinatown. It will bring you to somewhat of an understanding of the Chinese experience in San Francisco before you begin. Numbers 53–58 will give you some guidance and directions once you do. You'll also find a couple of Chinatown tours listed under number 90, although it's infinitely more fun to scout the area on your own. Just keep your eyes and nose open for the unusual (hint: you won't find it in the gift shops), be sure to poke into the side streets and dark alleys, and above all use your chopsticks!

4 GOLDEN GATE BRIDGE

Launched midst a thousand hopes and fears
Damned by a thousand hostile sneers
Yet ne'er its course was stayed
But ask of those who met the foe
Who stood alone when faith was low
Ask them the price they paid.

From "The Mighty Task is Done" by Joseph B. Strauss, Chief
Engineer of the Golden Gate Bridge

Looking at the majestic Golden Gate Bridge, you might find it hard to believe that San Francisco was once staunchly against the idea of stringing a golden necklace across the gate. The ferries that plied the Bay contended—correctly—that a bridge would run them out of business. Seamen were afraid of ships that would go bump in the night. The military conjured up visions of an enemy attack felling the bridge, trapping American war ships in the harbor. Environmentalists complained—weakly—of aesthetics, while anyone with an opinion contended that the ocean currents were too swift, the ocean floor too deep and the whole damn area too prone to earthquakes. Bitch, bitch, bitch.

Into the middle of the fracas stepped Joseph B. Strauss, bridge builder and poet, offering only the most magnificent structure ever built by the hands of man. Strauss would have been in deeper than a herring at high tide if he hadn't been able to deliver. He did. Consider: the Golden Gate Bridge virtually breathes. In a wind of 100 mph (not impossible), the midspan can swing out twenty-one feet in either direction. Under extreme conditions of load and temperature, the towers can hoist or drop the bridge by as much as ten feet. Clearly, Strauss knew what he was up against.

Joseph B. Strauss died in 1937, just seven months after he completed his masterpiece. He had one last word for the bridge's detractors:

> *The bridge which "could not be" and which "should not be,"*
> *which the War Department would not permit and which would ruin*
> *the beauty of the Golden Gate, stands before you in all its majestic*
> *splendor—in complete refutation of every attack on it. So there.*

7

GOLDEN GATE BRIDGE FACTS

The best way to enjoy the Golden Gate Bridge is to walk it, although just looking at it comes in a close second. The pedestrian walkway is open sunrise to sunset. It takes about one half hour to walk the bridge each way. You can easily catch a Golden Gate Transit bus to and from the bridge. Phone 332-6600 for schedule and information.

Total length of the bridge, (including approaches): 8,981 feet (1¾ miles)

Length of main span: 4,200 feet (which made it the longest single span suspension bridge in the world until 1964, when the Verrazano-Narrows Bridge connecting Brooklyn and Staten Island was opened, with a main span a scant 60 feet longer)

Width of bridge: 90 feet (six lanes and two pedestrian walkways)

Height of towers: 746 feet above water (equal to 65 stories)

Bridge begun: 5 January 1933

Bridge completed: 27 April 1937, with the driving of a solid gold rivet

Bridge color: International Orange (the better to be seen in fog). Painting of the Golden Gate Bridge goes on continuously. It takes four years to apply one complete coat of paint.

Number of known suicides (up to 1980): 696

Number of known survivors (up to 1980): 12

Because most of the suicide leaps are made from the east side of the bridge, facing San Francisco, popular legend has it that most people want one last look at San Francisco before they jump. In fact, the west side of the bridge is closed to pedestrian traffic during the week, so the east side bears a disproportionate amount of the foot traffic . . . and the suicides.

Toll: $1, collected on southbound vehicles (entering San Francisco). The original toll in 1937 was 50¢ per car each way, plus 10¢ per passenger. Tolls dropped over the years until the hit a low of 50¢ in 1955, then started climbing again.

How the Golden Gate Bridge was named: The bridge takes its name from the strait it spans. The strait was named in 1848 by John Fremont, one of the early settlers in the area, who said: "To this Gate I give the name of 'Chrysophlae' or Golden Gate, for the same reason the harbor of Byzantium was called 'Chrysoceras,' or 'Golden Horn.' "

5 *Alcatraz*

The most popular paying attraction in San Francisco is Alcatraz, as well it should be. The modest cost (the tour itself is free, but the ride out will run you), the need for advance reservations and the occasional long lines are all perfectly reasonable in view of the historic attraction of the lonely island. You should make every effort to visit Alcatraz. Here's why:

Alcatraz has actually been open to the public only since 1973. For most of its history, Alcatraz has either been inaccessible, uninhabitable or inhospitable. The Indians believed it was haunted by evil spirits and wouldn't go near. When the Army first laid eyes on it in the nineteenth century, they reported bleakly of "a mass of rock with a very thin crust of bird manure on the surface." Since the rock was too big to blow up, the Army ran a flag up instead and saluted it. Fort Alcatraz thus became the first U.S. military fortification on the West Coast.

When the Civil War broke out a few years later, Fort Alcatraz dug in to defend against any foreign nations that might have designs on America's coast. No one attacked, however, so Alcatraz ended up serving its country (and casting its die) as a prison during the war. Later, Alcatraz was used to detain Indians during the Indian Wars, to house city prisoners after the 1906 Earthquake, and to confine POW's during World War I. Eventually, the Department of War disowned the island, but the Justice Department picked it up in 1934 to use as a Federal penitentiary. It was during the short penitentiary period in Alcatraz's history that "The Rock" earned its substantial reputation.

Make no mistake about it, Alcatraz was every bit as bad as it has been made out to be. It was an experiment in incarceration, a

"minimum privilege, maximum security" prison, intended only to break a man's spirit. The view back to San Francisco alone was enough to break his heart. Then, as today, the cold, shifting waters surrounding the island were virtually impossible to swim; the fog, wind and cold rolled over the island like snake eyes. A fitting epitaph was delivered by Frank C. Weatherman, the last inmate off the island, who said, "Alcatraz was never no good to nobody."

Eventually, Alcatraz became too expensive to keep up. By the time it was closed on 21 March 1963, the cost to house and feed each prisoner had risen to $90 a day. The island was quiet until November 1969, when a group of Indians began a two-year occupation of Alcatraz. The basis of their claim was a treaty arrangement that deeded all surplus government land back to the Indians. Pressed on the point, however, the U.S. Government decided that it had plans to turn Alcatraz into a national park. After 19 months on the cold and cranky island, the Indians were removed without incident. A year later, Alcatraz became a part of the Golden Gate National Recreation Area; in October 1973, it was opened to the public for guided tours by National Park Rangers.

The actual tour of Alcatraz is free, but there is a charge (reasonable) for the boat ride out. The tours leave from Fisherman's Wharf at Pier 43 (next to the sailing ship, The Balclutha). The boats leave every 45 minutes from 9 a.m.-5:15 p.m. (till only 3 p.m. in the winter). During the summer, you'll need upwards of three weeks to reserve weekend space and a week to reserve weekday space, although tickets are sold on a first-come-first-served basis every day until 10 a.m. The tour takes about two hours from dock to dock. It's cool and windy on Alcatraz, so dress warmly. Also, be sure to wear comfortable walking shoes. For more information, phone Harbor Carriers at 546-2805.

ALCATRAZ FACTS

Federal penitentiary years: 29 years from 1934-1963
Facilities: 336 single-prisoner cells, 42 solitary-confinement cells. The average prison population was about 250.

Minimum sentence: 5 years (but a prisoner still had to earn his way off the island with good behavior). The average stay on Alcatraz was nine years.

Rights: A prisoner on Alcatraz had only four: food, clothing, shelter, and medical attention.

Discipline: The severest was confinement in "The Hole," a cold, steel cell having no light. Prisoners could be held there as long as the warden saw fit, providing they were brought out to air at least one day out of twenty. Perhaps the harshest penalty of all, however, was the general prison policy from 1934 to 1940: no talking. Early prisoners remember sticking their heads into their toilets to hold sewer line conversations.

Deaths: 30 prisoners died on Alcatraz in 29 years.

Famous Prisoners: *Al Capone* arrived with the first shipment of prisoners in 1934. Popular belief is that he left a babbling idiot. In fact he did leave suffering from "mental disturbances," as the warden put it, but this was due largely to a case of syphilis he contacted as a youth. Capone did die a free man at the age of 48 in 1947.

When *Robert Stroud, "The Birdman of Alcatraz"* died, 54 of his 73 years had been spent in prison, 17 of those in solitary confinement at Alcatraz. While in prison, Stroud killed a guard and was sentenced to hang but was spared by President Woodrow Wilson, largely because of Stroud's pioneering work with birds. But most of Stroud's work was done at Leavenworth. He wrote but did no research while at Alcatraz.

Escapes: 39 prisoners tried to escape in 14 separate attempts. Of those, twenty-six were captured, seven were shot and killed, one drowned and two are presumed to have drowned. Another three are still unaccounted for. In 1962, Frank Morris and Clarence and John Anglin slipped off the island and probably made it to safety. Clint Eastwood's 1979 movie "Escape From Alcatraz" is about that attempt. Only one man is known for sure to have made it across the Bay to San Francisco. In 1962, John Paul Scott washed up under the Golden Gate Bridge after a successful swim from The Rock. He was, unfortunately, unconscious. Not knowing that he was in the middle of an escape attempt, some passersby called police. Scott was revived and returned to prison.

6 THE WORLD'S CROOKEDEST STREET

With any luck, you can still take a tumble down one of the most famous streets in the world—the 1000 block of Lombard Street, known as "The World's Crookedest Street." Truth is, however, the residents of Lombard Street have grown a little tired of the 24-hour commotion caused by their famous street and want to close it off to all but foot traffic. They've even gone so far as to try to slough their dubious distinction off onto another San Francisco street across town with the suspect reasoning that the six *tight* turns on Vermont Street qualify it over the eight lazy curves of Lombard as the world's crookedest.

The world thus far remains unmoved by their plea. However, if you want to make a Lombard Street resident very happy, simply hop the Hyde Street/Fisherman's Wharf cable car. It'll take you right past the summit of the street, where you can snap a picture or stroll down the famous flower-lined lane.

7 UNION STREET

If you had only a day or two to see San Francisco, you'd probably want to spend them at Fisherman's Wharf and in Chinatown. If you had a third day, however, you'd want to spend at least part of it on Union Street.

Union Street is San Francisco in full bloom. It's charming, romantic, o-so-Victorian and glamorous without being stuffy. It's a picture postcard view of the City, the one you're most likely to carry home with you.

Turn to page 126 for the unlikely rise of Union Street from cow pasture to haute couture, as well as for a few things to look for up and down the street.

8 Sausalito

One of San Francisco's most popular draws isn't even in San Francisco. Across the Golden Gate and over the Bay is Sausalito, a one-time small town that has managed to parlay its name and fame into a tourist bonanza. Over the years, people like Sally Stanford (*Lady of the House*), Jack London, Alan Watts, and Shel Silverstein have lived and played in Sausalito. Ironically, much of Sausalito's artist community has been chased out by the commercial developers who trade on their very reputation. But even though Sausalito has lost much of its small town ambience, it still retains most of its charm. Sausalito is fun and a good excuse for crossing the Golden Gate Bridge or for taking a ferry across the Bay. And its a great place to have lunch or dinner. Turn to page 160 for a brief history of Sausalito and for a few things to look for once you're there.

9 COIT TOWER

Coit Tower is one of San Francisco's most recognizable symbols, right up there with the Golden Gate Bridge and the cable car. From the top of the tower on Telegraph Hill you can see almost everything there is to see in San Francisco, including an eyeful of the Bay. Which is exactly why a telegraph station was located at the top of the hill in 1850

—to advise the young city of approaching ships. Then, for awhile, an observatory owned the top, served by its own cable car. Later, the top was converted into a scenic park for picnickers. What we have here is a hill with a little bit of history.

So it was that when city benefactor Lillie Hitchcock Coit left a sum of money to "beautify the city I have always loved," San Francisco jumped at the opportunity to add a crowning touch to Telegraph Hill. Miss Coit, a devoted fire chaser and honorary fireperson, intended that a statue depicting a couple of firemen caught in a random act of courage grace the hilltop. (That statue was cast, but was placed in Washington Square in North Beach instead.) The City had grander plans for the hilltop and Miss Coit's money, commissioning a "simple fluted shaft" for Telegraph Hill. The fact that it resembles an elongated fire hydrant makes it look as though the irrepressible Miss Coit had a hand in the design. She didn't. After some initial misgivings, San Francisco took Coit Tower to its heart, and the two have since become as tight as corn on the cob.

Shortly after Coit Tower was finished, the federal government began to finance public art projects. Coit Tower's inside walls were selected for an ambitious mural depicting "Aspects of Life in California, 1934." Twenty-five artists were used to revive the art of fresco painting, in which earth colors are applied directly to the wet plaster. The artists also interjected some of their own leftist thoughts into the work, causing such a fuss that Coit Tower had to be closed for a year while the murals were doctored.

Coit Tower is open seven days a week, 9 a.m.-4:30 p.m. The tower is free but there's a small charge for the elevator ride to the top. The frescoes are on display daily from 2-4 p.m. Phone 362-8037.

10 GOLDEN GATE PARK

So what's so special about a park? Plenty, in the case of Golden Gate Park. For starters, it's huge: it rolls out of the Pacific to cut a swath of trees and grass half-a-mile wide and three-miles long through the heart of San Francisco's most condensed residential district. It has something for just about everyone: museums, gardens, concerts, playgrounds, lakes, buffaloes, roller skating and a lot of places to just lose yourself in thought. And something always seems to be happening in the park. Back before the turn of the century, San Francisco hosted a World's Fair there. For years the football Forty-Niners made their home off to one side of the park in cozy Kezar Stadium. During the height of the Haight Ashbury, the hippies threw feeds and concerts in the park "Panhandle," gathered en masse for the famous Human Be-In, even named a hill—Hippie Hill, but of course.

Yup, Golden Gate Park is easily the equal of its city, and that's going some. If you have a Sunday to spend in San Francisco, you won't find a better place to spend it. Turn to page 144 for a few ideas.

DON'T MISS

11 DON'T YOU DARE LEAVE TOWN WITHOUT HAVING AN IRISH COFFEE AT THE BUENA VISTA___

Joe DiMaggio and Levi's notwithstanding, Irish Coffee is probably the most popular San Francisco export since gold. The whiskey and coffee drink was first introduced to America in 1952 at the Buena Vista, then merely a thriving Fisherman's Wharf bar. Today Irish Coffee is a staple of every bar in the country and its humble birthplace is a National Historic Landmark. You simply haven't done San Francisco until you've had an Irish Coffee at the "BV."

Understand, the Buena Vista didn't actually invent the drink. That had been done some years before in Ireland, which is where Stanton Delaplane, a columnist for the *San Francisco Chronicle*, discovered it one wet evening while waiting in the Shannon airport bar. He jotted down the recipe from bartender Joe Sheridan and brought it back to the Buena Vista. Unfortunately, the "BV" bartenders couldn't quite duplicate the drink Delaplane had tasted in Ireland. Chief of the two problems facing the intrepid pioneers was finding a whiskey that was submissive to the coffee. They cracked the case with Tullamore Dew, an Irish whiskey that adds almost no taste to the coffee. (Today the Buena Vista receives their Tullamore Dew in boxcar loads, a discriminating portion of which they set aside to be bottled under their own imprint and sold at the nearby Cannery Gourmet Shop.)

The other problem was getting the cream collar to set just so at the top of the drink (whipped cream is a serious breach of taste). The secret is to use two day-old cream—still fresh, mind you, but thick enough to roll lazily off the spoon and lie obligingly on top of the coffee.

Over the years the "BV" has upped their output to some 600,000 glasses of Irish Coffee a year, making them one of the most wildly successful bars in the world. You'll see why when you get there. Just be sure that you do. And preferably early, since they fill up fast.

The Buena Vista is at 2765 Hyde Street (corner of Beach Street), across the street from the Hyde Street cable car turnaround. They're open seven days a week, 9 a.m.-2 a.m. Phone 474-5044.

12 HANG OUT AT CITY LIGHTS BOOKSTORE

City Lights Bookstore in North Beach is just about the funkiest, friendliest and most famous bookstore in America. For nearly three decades the cramped, misshapen bookstore has been a catalyst for some of the most original thoughts and thinkers of our time, including Allen Ginsberg, Jack Kerouac, Neal Cassady, Michael McClure and the captain himself, Lawrence Ferlinghetti.

City Lights came to be back in the early 1950s. Ferlinghetti came to San Francisco in 1951 because, he says, "it was the only place in the country where you could get decent wine cheap." But when he went looking for a hip bookstore, he found that "there was no place to walk into to browse, no place to talk to people, to just hang out." So he created one, appropriating the name from the Charlie Chaplin film. For awhile, Ferlinghetti published a magazine under the City Lights logo, but he subsequently gave that up for a much more successful book publishing company.

City Lights Books became a cause célèbre in 1956 when San Francisco police ran Ferlinghetti up on obscenity charges for publishing Ginsberg's snarling diatribe, "Howl." The media moved in on City Lights, San Francisco and the "beatniks" with a consuming curiosity. *Life* magazine even gave the ensuing trial the full picture-story treatment. In the end, "Howl" was judged to be hardly obscene, but the attention showered down on North Beach and the "beats" sent the whole scene into furious retreat and near oblivion.

Today, City Lights remains as a high-water mark of the incredible "beat" chapter in San Francisco's history. Ferlinghetti still tends to his store and it remains the same funky hangout he intended it to be, in spite of a 1977 expansion into a sunlit wing. If you want to find out what else is left over from the beat era, check out number 30 for a map and chronology of the short-lived Beat Generation.

City Lights is in the heart of North Beach at 261 Columbus Avenue, near the intersection of Broadway. It's open Mon.-Thur. 10 a.m.-midnight, Fri.-Sat. 10 a.m.-1 a.m., and Sunday noon-midnight. Phone 362-8193.

13 CAROL DODA

Over in the heart of San Francisco's notorious Broadway district in a
tacky club that serves watered drinks, a legitimate San Francisco
legend holds forth. On the night of 19 June 1964, Carol Doda
wiggled into a Rudi Gernreich topless bathing suit, climbed onto the
stage of The Condor Nightclub and blew the top off of America.
That night just happened to be the opening night of the 1964 Repub-
lican Convention being held in San Francisco, and the nation's scru-
tiny made Carol Doda an overnight sensation. She copped even more
attention when she upped her bust size to 44 inches with silicone
implants. Those, on top of a trim 22-inch waist and 36-inch hips,
have made Carol Doda a sight to see, and one that you shouldn't miss.

You'll find her most nights of the week in the now "World Famous
Condor Nightclub" at Broadway and Columbus, beneath the famous
flashing neon nipples. Carol's not in every night, so call ahead at
392-4443 (but don't necessarily expect the truth).

A NIGHT WITH CAROL DODA

*"Ladies and gentlemen, 15 minutes till the sensational Miss Carol
Doda, just 15 minutes till showtime. . . ."*

The red velvet curtain parts and you enter "The World Famous
Condor Nightclub." You quickly realize that no matter what, Carol
Doda is always just 15 minutes away. You sit through a seemingly
endless succession of strippers, each executing a rote routine of tired
bumps and perfunctory grinds. At length, the announcer assures you
that it is time for Miss Carol Doda. A hush descends on the room.

Suddenly a huge brass band strikes up from out of nowhere, and the footlights go beserk as if filled with the knowledge of what is about to be. As quickly as you can count to 44-22-36, Carol Doda is upon you, whirling and swirling about the stage in a pink chiffon haze.

"I think of myself as an entertainer. I like to make contact with my audience, talk to them, find out where they're at."

She grips the microphone and prowls the stage, bantering with the audience, most of whom are too wide-eyed and tongue-tied to do much more than blurt out the name of their home town.

"I have a sense of humor. I like to have fun with my audience. And I can also sing. I've had ten years of voice lessons. I'm really proud of that."

And sing she can, though you'd never know it to hear her at The Condor. Her husky-sweet voice falls limp and lifeless from the hapless sound system and is trampled over by the mystery band that wails away incessantly from the sound booth in the back.

"I miss the way they used to strip in the old days. Girls now days just take their clothes off, boom, boom, boom. No class."

"Do you have an idol, some stripper that you admire?"

"No . . . well, yes. I used to love watching old Fred Astaire movies. I just loved the way he moved. I can do all that, all the 'la ta ta'. . . ."

Carol prances back and forth across the stage. Then, with a sudden toss of her platinum mane and a wink, she turns woman-child. She wrinkles her nose and squeals innocently: "I think I'll do something very unusual now. Don't look, because I'm going to . . .take my clothes off."

23

24

"I've worked at The Condor since I was 17. I wasn't even 21 yet when I went topless. I was a cocktail waitress, very entertaining. I would sing, tell jokes. People used to come in just so I would wait on them. One day my boss said: 'This is your new costume.' It was a topless bathing suit. That night I went on. I said, 'Y'know, with this costume I can't wait on tables anymore.' And I never have since."

The chiffon topping floats to her feet. Her sequinned dress slides slowly down her firm body, leaving only a G-string and a top. She cups one breast, then the other. With an oomph and an eye she reaches for her top and unclasps it. You blink back your disbelief and then, there you are, face to face with . . . THEM!

"I was arrested a year and a half later. I didn't even know it was coming, can you believe that? The Condor knew the arrest was coming, but they wanted it for the publicity. I didn't like going to jail. It hurt me. I was crying."

Wait a minute! Is this the same Carol Doda, sultry titan of temptation? The woman who single-bodily introduced topless and bottomless to a world already insane? Could it be that her pretty Cheshire grin masks the soul of a pussycat?

"I'm naive, sure. People ask me why I still do what I do. I enjoy it, I really do. I'm an entertainer. I like putting on a good show. It makes me feel good if people have a good time. I try to do a family show. I'm into the family scene, y'know. I never had one of my own, really. I guess I've always felt alone a lot."

She mounts her piano, and with a shake and a shimmy she disappears into the ceiling. The mystery band is by now in a tizzy, the footlights lost in delirium. You drink up and quickly make your way to the exit, past the red velvet curtain and back onto the streets of North Beach.

"Ladies and gentlemen, 15 minutes till the lovely Miss Carol Doda, just 15 minutes till showtime. . . ."

14 SEE THE SITE OF SAN FRANCISCO'S MOST FAMOUS MURDER

The San Francisco night was as cold and clammy as a three-day corpse. Sam Spade turned his collar up and stared blindly down the dark alley as a policeman ticked off the details. Miles Archer had been shot once, point blank. The body was found halfway down Burritt Street, a small, residential alley. Archer's own gun was still holstered, his overcoat still buttoned. No one in the neighborhood heard the shot nor saw the murderer leave the alley. It didn't hardly make sense, did it Spade, for a seasoned detective like Archer to tail someone down a blind alley with his own heat on his hip? Spade nodded in agreement, but he was thinking different. Archer was no Einstein. He'd tried his tired Casanova on the wrong Jezabel and paid the Piper. But Spade knew he would have to find the Benedict Arnold who did this before she pulled a Houdini. Besides, it was bad for business to let your partner's murderer get away.

Confusing? Hell, it's only the beginning. For you see, the murder of Miles Archer takes place in the pages of Dashiell Hammett's hard-boiled classic, *The Maltese Falcon*. During the late 1920s, Hammett was the unquestioned master of the detective fiction novel, *The Maltese Falcon* his masterpiece. He wrote it while living in San Francisco and used the City as a backdrop. Most of the locations in the book actually exist, including the Burritt Street setting where Miles Archer was shot. Not so coincidentally, Hammett wrote the book at 20 Monroe Street, another small alleyway just across the street from Burritt. To get to either, go to Union Square. Head north on Stockton Street for two blocks, then climb the stairs on either side of the Stockton Street Tunnel to Bush Street. Just past the Tunnel Top Bar on Bush Street you'll run into Burritt Street, now marked by a plaque that reads:

> On approximately this spot
> Miles Archer,
> Partner of Sam Spade,
> Was done in by
> Brigid O'Shaughnessy.

If you really want to get into some serious Hammett trivia, head down to John's Grill near the Powell Street cable car turnaround. John's Grill was one of Hammett's favorite restaurants in real life, and Hammett even had Spade stop off for an "order of chops, baked potatoes and sliced tomatoes" during a tense scene in *The Maltese Falcon*. Because of that, the upstairs of the restaurant has been canonized "The Maltese Falcon Room." The walls are lined with stills from the Bogart movie (including the classic scene in which Spade sends O'Shaughnessy over), autographed copies of Hammett's books, all manners of books and articles about him, and even a replica of the famous black bird itself.

John's Grill is also one of the best restaurants in the City. It's at 63 Ellis Street, off Powell Street. It's open Mon.-Sat. 10 a.m.-10 p.m. Phone 986-0069.

15 DON'T MISS THE CABLE CAR MUSEUM

For one thing, it's hard to miss. Both of the Fisherman's Wharf cable car lines pass right by it. It's also the only one of its kind in the world, is genuinely interesting, and is free to boot. So, go.

Inside the Cable Car Museum you'll look down onto the very heart of the cable car system—three 14-foot wheels that turn the cables at a steady nine miles an hour. The present machinery is an exact duplicate of the original 1887 works. Elsewhere in the museum you'll see the very first cable car that inventor Andrew Hallidie piloted into history on 1 August 1873, as well as models of every type of cable car that has ever run the streets of San Francisco. You'll enjoy this one.

The Cable Car Museum is at 1201 Mason Street (corner of Washington Street). To get there, just hop either the Powell-Mason or Powell-Hyde line and tell the gripman where you're going. It's open Mon.-Sun. 10 a.m.-6 p.m. (shorter hours in the winter). Phone 474-1887. Free.

16 GO BEACH BLANKET BANANAS

Snow White warbles while a bucket of dirty dishes wobbles precariously atop her head. Tables sprout legs and do a jig and hamburgers find their voices and break into song. Don't bother trying to understand it. But do try to get tickets for absolutely the most delightful show in town. "Beach Blanket Babylon Goes To The Stars" may just be the place in San Francisco where you leave your heart.

"BBBGTTS" is a G-rated, nonsensical musical comedy that was born on the streets of San Francisco. It all began when a couple of off-center friends combined their unique talents to form "Rent-A-Freak," street happeners. That was back in 1969, and the tale has grown so in the telling that "Beach Blanket Babylon" is now firmly ensconced in a North Beach theatre. *People* magazine was so charmed by it that they spent two pages on it in a 1979 issue. Even though the show is usually sold out weeks in advance, don't let it stop you from calling for tickets. And don't put yourself above attempting a bribe, either. "Beach Blanket Babylon" is well worth it.

"Beach Blanket Babylon Goes To The Stars" plays at the Club Fugazi, 678 Green Street in North Beach. Performances are held Wednesday through Sunday, with a late show on Friday and Saturday. Phone 421-4222 for reservations.

17 VISIT A PLACE WHERE EVERY THING YOU KNOW IS WRONG

To be perfectly honest, the Exploratorium is a museum of science.

Boring, right?

Wrong! The Exploratorium is a marvel for child and adult alike. It's a hands-on museum with over 400 exhibits, all trading loosely on the laws of nature and science. The idea is, in the words of its creator, to never feel "compelled to decide whether you're supposed to learn something or enjoy yourself." Happily, you never are, although you may find that your brain is no longer the boss.

The Exploratorium is at 3610 Lyon Street, in the Palace of Fine Arts. It's open Wed.-Fri. 1-5 p.m., Sat.-Sun. 11 a.m.-5 p.m., and Wednesday evening 7-9:30 p.m. (shorter hours in the winter). Phone 563-7337. Donation requested.

18 BART

BART is the twenty-first century come to roost beneath the streets of San Francisco. Never mind what you think about subways, mass transit and progress, BART is about as pleasant and painless as stainless steel has a right to be. It has elevated the once tawdry business of shepherding commuters from place to place into a dignified art befitting the jewel of American cities, and that's going some.

BART stands for Bay Area Rapid Transit. It's 71 miles of track and train that stitch San Francisco and two East Bay counties together (Marin County to the north bowed out because the Golden Gate Bridge wouldn't bear the additional weight). The whole system took 23 years to plan and execute, eventually costing the taxpayers of San Francisco and the U.S. a staggering $1.6 billion, half of that in overruns. Even at that, the first train was five years late. It took nine years alone to think and sink the heart of BART to the bottom of the Bay—the 3.6 mile Transbay Tube, which connects San Francisco with Oakland. Today, the trip through The Tube takes a mere six minutes at speeds approaching BART's top end of 80 mph.

Here's what you need to know in order to take BART:

If you want just a spin without actually getting off the train (outside of San Francisco most of BART's route is above ground), then head straight for the station attendant and buy an Excursion Pass. This pass allows you to ride for three hours (excluding rush hours during the week) for only $1, providing you enter and exit at the same station.

Going from one point to another is a different matter. Be sure to bring plenty of crisp, one dollar bills (the ticket machines are very finicky), and check with the station attendant or fellow passengers if you need help.

Children under five ride for free. There is no smoking allowed anywhere within the entry gates or on the waiting platform or trains. BART runs Mon.-Sat. 6 a.m.-midnight, and Sunday 9 a.m.-midnight. For more information, phone 788-BART.

Where BART goes:

BART trains are referred to by their final destination and not by their major stops. Thus, the underground currency

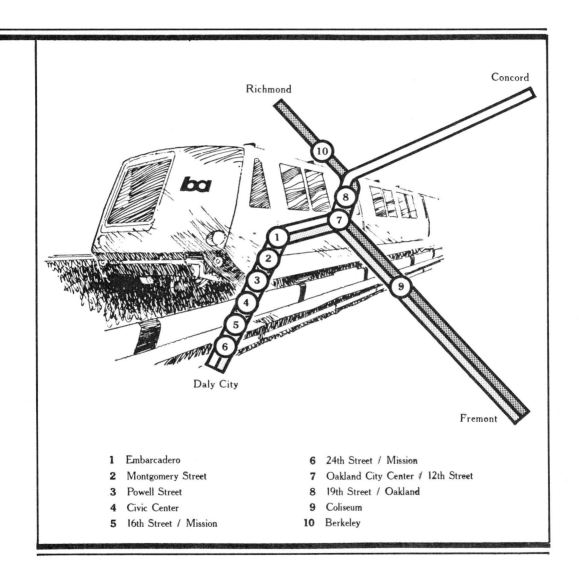

1	Embarcadero	**6**	24th Street / Mission
2	Montgomery Street	**7**	Oakland City Center / 12th Street
3	Powell Street	**8**	19th Street / Oakland
4	Civic Center	**9**	Coliseum
5	16th Street / Mission	**10**	Berkeley

isn't "San Francisco" and "Oakland," but rather "Daly City," "Concord," "Fremont," and "Richmond." Don't worry—there are plenty of maps on the waiting platform and in the trains, and always a helpful passenger at your side.

Here are the stops of interest to you along BART's way:

SAN FRANCISCO

The Embarcadero The first stop in San Francisco for trains coming from Oakland and the last for trains heading into The Tube. Lets you off at the base of California and Market Streets, near the Embarcadero Center and a few steps from the California cable car line, which will, in turn, take you through Chinatown and over Nob Hill.

Montgomery Street Lets you off at Market and Montgomery Streets, in the heart of the Financial District. This is BART's busiest station.

Powell Street Lets you out onto Hallidie Plaza, the area around the Powell Street cable car turnaround.

Union Square is just upstairs. You can pick up a cable car here and ride to Fisherman's Wharf. Probably the most convenient station to get to and from if you're BARTing for recreation.

Civic Center Lets you out onto the Civic Center complex on the fringes of downtown San Francisco. Not terribly much to do here.

16th Street Mission and 24th Street Mission The two Mission Street exits. Either one will put you in the middle of the interesting Mission Street action. San Francisco's oldest building, the Mission Dolores, is just three blocks west of the 16th Street exit, on 16th and Dolores.

OAKLAND

Oakland City Center/12th Street and 19th Street Puts you on one side or the other of the core downtown area of Oakland.

Coliseum If you find yourself going to the Oakland Coliseum or Stadium for a sporting or music event, you can BART right to the stadium. Beats every other way of going.

BERKELEY

Berkeley The best reason to go to the East Bay. The University of California Berkeley campus is a couple of blocks east of the Berkeley exit and is a lot of fun to browse, shop and eat. If you get turned around, just ask the inevitable street people for directions.

ONLY IN SAN FRANCISCO

19 GIVE US THIS DAY OUR DAILY BARD

Forget the coffee and forego the shower. Around these parts, everyone wakes up to Herb Caen.

Who is Herb Caen? He's a columnist for the morning *Chronicle*. He's arguably the best in the business, but he's unquestionably Mr. San Francisco. Like his City, Caen is folksy, provincial, nostalgic, a bit set in his ways . . . and proud. Proud of the fog, the cable cars, the hills and everything else that makes San Francisco unique. He is the mood and conscience of the City, given to understated profundity . . . and always three dots.

It is said that one word in Herb Caen is worth 10,000 pictures. He coined the word "beatnik" and has positioned himself square in the front ranks in the war on "Frisco." Herb Caen's greatest achievement, however, has been to make San Francisco at long-last proud of its fog, for years thought to be worse than the curse and a whole lot more frequent. His city serenades, "fog creeping through the bridge pieces," have become a standard part of his repertoire, usually reserved for Sundays and Special Occasions.

For your own purposes, you'll get along quite well in San Francisco if you sprinkle your conversation with an item or two from that morning's column, adhere to Caen's edict to "Dress conservatively, cling to the outside of cable cars and make bad jokes about Los Angeles" . . . and never, say never, say "Frisco."

20 Taste the Beer That San Francisco Made Famous

Anchor Steam Beer is a case of a beer that couldn't be brewed anywhere else, to San Francisco's great credit and infinite pleasure. Each bottle is a liquid lesson in San Francisco history, if you will (or simply one of the most honest beers in the world if you won't).

Here's how it came to be:

One of the most severely felt hardships of pioneer life in San Francisco had to be the lack of beer. Since everything, including ice for the brewing process, had to be shipped around the Horn, traditional beer was just too expensive to brew. So, San Francisco came up with a very untraditional beer that would ferment naturally in the cool climate here. Thus was born "steam" beer (a misnomer, it probably was first used to refer to the lively head that's a result of the natural carbonation), the only beer native to the U.S. Being the only beer available, steam breweries naturally flourished on the West Coast, reaching a peak of 27 here in San Francisco. Mechanical refrigeration trimmed that number to seven by the time of Prohibition. After Prohibition was repealed, the Anchor Steam Brewery was the only one to reopen; but by 1965, it too was about to go under.

Enter Fritz Maytag (yup, that Maytag), then a student at Stanford University, who heard of the imminent closing and went over for a historic last look at a unique brewing process. He ended up buying the brewery and learning how to brew beer. In that order. Today he has a small brewery in the black and a beer of integrity. Not bad for a kid from a family that made their name dabbling in quite a different kind of suds.

Anchor Steam tastes a little different than popular "light" American beers, because it's made with only the traditional beer-making ingredients: barley, malt, hops, water, and yeast. No preservatives and no

35

additives, and none of the corn and rice that makes popular American beers "light" in color and taste. Anchor Steam is still "krausened," or naturally fermented, like champagne. In all, the meticulous process takes about a month to complete from barley to bottle.

Anchor Steam offers tours of its brewery but doesn't really encourage them because of its small staff. If you're a connoisseur of the art, you can arrange for an informative guided tour by calling 863-1495. The tour is free. It ends up in the Anchor Steam Hospitality Room, amidst an interesting assortment of brewing memorabilia from around the world.

21 GET A TATTOO

If you were thinking about taking back a suntan as evidence of your stay in San Francisco, forget it. You've probably noticed that it's too cold to take off much more than your coat.

So how about taking back a tattoo? It won't peel and is more personal and lasts a lot longer than a suntan. And you couldn't pick a better place to go under the needle than right here in San Francisco. Not only do some of the world's best and most famous tattoo artists work here, but the whole sixties renaissance of the art can be traced to a little walk-up studio next to the bus depot in a seedy part of San Francisco.

It was in Lyle Tuttle's studio that Janis Joplin had a flower bracelet tattooed on her left wrist and a red heart etched above her left breast. When she let the world know about them on a Dick Cavett Show appearance, other rock stars began stopping off at Tuttle's studio to have work done, including the Allman Brothers (Gregg has three),

Joan Baez, Peter Fonda, Anita Pointer and Cher, who has a rose and butterfly tattooed on her posterior.

If your body is ready to make its statement, here's where to take it:

LYLE TUTTLE

Tuttle is the acknowledged titan of the tattoo. Tuttle himself is tattooed from neck to ankle (stopping short of his extremities because he feels tattooes are sort of a personal thing). He's been featured in a number of magazines, including *Life* and *Esquire*. He still works out of the tiny walk-up studio that Janis Joplin went to. It's at 30 Seventh Street, just off Market Street. Open Mon.-Sat. noon-midnight, Sunday noon-6 p.m. Phone 864-9798.

MISSION LIGHTS STUDIO

Mission Lights Tattoo Studio is at 3507 Mission Street. Open Tue.–Sun. Phone 285-3376.

PICTURE MAGAZINE

Pat Martynuik runs this one. He's one of the best, selling his designs to tattoo artists around the world. He's in his studio most of the time, but call ahead for an appointment. Picture Magazine is at 3940 Geary Boulevard. Open Mon.-Sat. noon-midnight, Sunday noon-6 p.m. Phone 668-7377.

REALISTIC TATTOO

Ed Hardy, who runs Realistic Tattoo, was voted the tattoo artist of the year in 1977. He works out of Realistic Tattoo by appointment only, seven days a week. Realistic Tattoo is at 2535 Van Ness Avenue. Phone 928-0910.

22 TAKE HOME A LOAF OF CENTURY-OLD BREAD

Sourdough bread is Mother Nature's original clone. Take a chunk of today's sourdough, add water and flour, let it sit overnight and presto —you have tomorrow's sourdough.

Just like with fine wine, the longer this process goes on the better the bread gets. Which is one certifiable reason why San Francisco's sourdough bread is acknowledged as "the master bread-maker's bread," the very best in the world. Most of the bakeries in town have been cloning their sourdough daily for over a century. The oldest, Boudin Bakery, traces its sourdough all the way back to 1849, the year it was introduced to California by the European and Mexican prospectors who found it a whole lot easier to breed their bread than to grow it up in the diggins.

But that's not the only reason San Francisco's sourdough is the best. In 1970, a $49,000 Federal study of San Francisco's sourdough managed to isolate a previously unidentified microorganism, which was named "Lactobacillus Sanfrancisco." The net result of the study was to prove that you can take the sourdough out of San Francisco, but you can't take the San Francisco out of the sourdough.

If you went to know a little more about the mysterious sourdough process, peak into the picture windows of the Boudin Bakery, 160 Jefferson Street, in Fisherman's Wharf. They bake from 8 a.m.-2 p.m., seven days a week, but the best time to look in is at 8:30 a.m., when they mix the dough. Don't expect to see too much, however. The bakers around here are only too happy to keep the sourdough process somewhat of a mystery, thereby perpetuating the mystique of San Francisco's sourdough. Phone 928-1849.

23 SEE THE MAN WHO GAVE BIRTH TO THE BLUES

The rags-to-britches story of Levi Strauss is one of the most famous legends from early San Francisco. When young Levi landed in San Francisco in 1850, he carried with him the requisite high hopes — and a load of canvas he hoped to turn into tents. "Should have brought pants instead," the miners scoffed. "Pants don't wear worth a hoot up in the diggins."

So Levi quickly fashioned his canvas into pants. They were such a hit that he stayed in the business, eventually switching from canvas to a tough, blue cotton fabric loomed in Nimes, France, and called "serge de Nimes" (hence "denim"). Well, to make a long story short, Levi Strauss had a bit of success with his denim jeans, and the company that bears his name is today one of the largest manufacturers of clothes in the world.

A small museum in the world headquarters of Levi Strauss traces the modest blue jean from its Humble Beginnings to the present. Also on display are a pair of the smallest jeans made by Levi, and the largest — a 76" waist (if you measure up you can have a pair, free).

The Levi Strauss & Co. History Room is in Two Embarcadero Center. It's open Mon.-Fri. 10 a.m.-4 p.m. Phone 544-7224. Free.

24 TURN ON & TUNE IN KSAN

If you grew up with the late, lost art of progressive rock radio, then KSAN in San Francisco is your musical forebearer. It's the grand-daddy of FM rockers and a true American classic.

If the name is familiar, it's probably because of the national exposure KSAN has received over the years from blood-relative *Rolling Stone* (Senior Editor Ben Fong-Torres used to pull down a regular airshift) and because of KSAN's larger-than-life muse, Tom Donahue. "Big Daddy" Donahue was already something of an AM legend in San Francisco when the thought occurred to him, one stoned birthday evening, that his favorite groups—the Grateful Dead, Janis Joplin, The Doors—weren't being played on the radio. So he gathered up his records and a few of his favored friends, conspired with KMPX, then a failing FM station at the north end of the dial, and revolution-ized radio. His jocks went on long, stoney "sets" and talked in real voices about things that mattered. Listeners responded with records, drugs and undying devotion. It was all too much for the station owner, so the staff walked in "The Great Hippie Strike" for the AAFIFMWW—The Amalgamated American Federation of In-ternational FM Workers of the World, North Beach Local 1. The hippies lost the strike, but on 21 May 1968—another of Donahue's birthday's—they won the war. They ran the freak flag up at classical station KSFR, changed the call letters to KSAN and plugged them-selves into the unfolding dream.

Under Donahue, KSAN created some of the most vital and valid radio in America. It became the station of record for the entire rock industry. Bands flocked to KSAN's side, bearing tickets and trinkets. KSAN, in turn, helped launch the diverse likes of the Grateful Dead, Peter Frampton, Elvis Costello and Blondie. The SLA sent a couple of Patty Hearst communiques to KSAN, including the infamous "Tania" photo.

The times changed, however. Tom Donahue died in 1975. KSAN remained a beacon of free-form originality throughout the Great Disco Menace of the late '70s, but was toppled from within in 1979. When KSAN's parent company imported a gaggle of geeks from Los

Angeles to regroove the station, the KSAN staff walked for a second time, this time for good.

Then, in 1980, KSAN's pioneering rock format was plowed under and replaced with a hybrid country format. You'll still find the late, lamented "Ace of the Airwaves" at 95 on the FM dial. The multi-colored KSAN building still stands out against the drab Financial District at 345 Sansome Street.

25 SEE THE WORLD'S MOST AMAZING MOUSTACHE

It starts beneath his nose and then just *goes*. It clears his cheeks at about three inches, turns north in a graceful loop, curls up and in and finally around into two of the cutest little "o's" this side of Chef Boy-ar-dee. It looks for all the world like his nose has sprouted wings and is about to take flight, but actually it's only Milt Harper's moustache. Harper began The Darn Thing back in 1968, and he's kept it up through War, Peace, Resignation, several recessions, and Disco—all the while seeing to the gargantuan task of keeping it cleaned, waxed and out of the way of innocent bystanders.

Now, a man with a 10-inch handlebar moustache obviously isn't looking for a lot of privacy. Harper has taken to attending celebrity events and having his mug snapped with the likes of Bob Hope, Clint Eastwood, George C. Scott, Liza Minelli, and Vincent Price. The pictures are on display at Harper's tiny business on Market Street, as is Harper when he's in his picture-window office. Take a peek in.

Milt Harper's business is called the Nite Life Dinner Club, It's in the Orpheum Theatre Building, Eighth and Market Streets, downtown, near the Civic Center BART exit.

26 Flood Your Buds

Ever since 1920, San Francisco has had a sweet tooth for a native ice cream delight called the *It's-It*. Back then it was only available at Playland-at-the-Beach, an ocean-side amusement park. When Playland went under in 1972, San Francisco was naturally concerned that the *It's-It* would follow it into oblivion. It did, in fact, but only for a year. A small company stepped in to purchase the name and the rights, and began making the chocolate-covered ice cream sandwiches in the time-honored way: by hand, with all natural ingredients. Nowadays they're a staple of self-respecting grocery stores and theatres throughout San Francisco and northern California. You'll find them in the ice cream section, lying in frozen repose next to the crowd of lesser ice cream treats.

NOTE: When selecting your first *It's-It*, it's very important that you resist the temptation to grab the top sandwich and split. Be calm! Since *It's-Its* are made by hand, no two are exactly alike. Feel each one out in turn, looking for the plumpest and hardest. If an *It's-It* isn't frozen in the freezer, it will become mushy in your mouth, and the *It's-It*, like all adult pleasures, is meant to be eaten, not slurped.

When you're satisfied that you've found the right *It's-It* for you, sit back to enjoy a taste of San Francisco tradition. And welcome to San Francisco.

27 TRY A TASTE OF TRADITION

If you do much sampling among San Francisco's bounty of restaurants, you'll probably come across a curious combination of scrambled eggs, hamburger, spinach, mushrooms and onions. This deservedly humble concoction is known around these parts as a "Joe's Special," although some restaurants have been known to affix their own moniker to it. (One large chain of restaurants even serves it as a "San Francisco Special.") Whatever, "Joe's Special" has become something of a lunchtime legend in San Francisco, although the exact why and wherefore is a little sketchy.

This much is known: the dish was created at New Joe's Restaurant, an eatery that held out in the heart of San Francisco's Broadway action until the mid-'60s. According to the legend, a late-night party came into New Joe's requesting a midnight snack. Fresh out of just about everything, Joe obligingly whipped up the last of his supplies—guess what—creating in the process a dish that wasn't quite scrambled eggs and wasn't quite an omelette but was . . . well, a "Joe's Special."

A notorious soft touch for tradition, San Francisco kept up the popular lunch even after New Joe closed his doors. Here are ten places where you can still taste the tradition today:

Hoffman's Grill   619 Market Street (Downtown) 421-1467
John's Grill   63 Ellis Street (Downtown) 986-0069
Little Joe's and Baby Joe's   325 Columbus (North Beach) 982-7639
Mama's   Three locations: 1701 Stockton Street (North Beach) 362-6241; 1177 California Street (Nob Hill) 928-1004; Macy's, Stockton and O'Farrell Streets (Downtown) 391-3790
Original Joe's   144 Taylor Street (Tenderloin District) 775-4877

Polo's Famous Restaurant   34 Mason Street (Tenderloin District) 362-7719

Trinity Joe's   Market at 8th Street (Downtown) 552-6333

Vanessi's   498 Broadway (North Beach) 421-0890

Washington Square Bar and Grill   1707 Powell Street (North Beach) 982-8123

Zim's   A variety of locations around the City. Call 921-7505 for the restaurant nearest you.

NOTE: A "Joe's Special" will naturally taste better at a "Joe's" restaurant. "Joe's" are an indigenous San Francisco restaurant form, distinguished by their hearty Italian fare and countertop ambience. Other than that, no two "Joe's" are related.

28 GET A PIECE OF THE ROCK

Bill Graham and rock are about as synonymous as Babe Ruth and baseball, so you'd figure that when Graham puts his name on a "rock shop" it would be a runaway success. You'd be absolutely right.

The Rock Shop is basically a T-shirt, poster and paraphernalia store, with a few discernible Graham edges. There are copies of many of the original Fillmore posters (now collector's items), pictures from some of the best shows down through the years, a few candid shots of Bill and his famous friends, and souvenirs from such grateful Graham-produced acts as Bob Dylan, Led Zeppelin and the Rolling Stones.

If you don't have time to do a full tour of San Francisco's magnificent Rock Country, Bill Graham's Rock Shop is a colorful counter-culture compendium. It's at 1333 Columbus (in Fisherman's Wharf, across from the Beach Street entrance to The Cannery). Phone 673-4970. Open Mon.-Sat., 10 a.m.-6 p.m., Sunday, 11 a.m.-6 p.m.

ODYSSEYS AND PILGRIMAGES

29 Barbary Coast

For all of its well-publicized transgressions, modern-day San Francisco has never even come close to equalling the complete and utter moral bankruptcy of the infamous Barbary Coast. The Barbary Coast was so bad, in fact, that at least three words had to be invented to describe evils that simply hadn't existed before. One of those words is *hoodlum*, after the command of a gang leader to "huddle 'em," or close ranks when confronted by police. The frequent practice of drugging unsuspecting sailors and then selling them off to ship captains in need of a crew became known as *shanghaiing*, after a common destination. The drug-laced drink administered to the victims was called a *Mickey Finn*, named for its inventor, Michael Finn, a discredited Scotch chemist plying his trade here.

The Barbary Coast existed in one form or another for almost seventy of San Francisco's young and impetuous years, from 1849 to 1917. It developed around a small colony of Chileno whores who set up their tents along what was then the waterfront at Broadway and Pacific Streets. The action never moved very far from that spot. The area was first called Sydney Town, after its unrepentant population of escaped convicts and ticket-of-leave criminals from the British penal colony in Australia. They arrived in direct defiance of American law, which was about as much mind as they ever paid it. Between 1849 and 1855, for example, San Francisco averaged two murders a night, most of which occurred within the criminal confines of Sydney Town. Eventually, though, Sydney Town was diluted by dregs from the rest of the world. Around the mid-1860s, it began to be called the Barbary Coast by sailors impressed with a lawless viciousness unknown outside of Africa's Barbary Coast. The area was directly responsible for the formation of the infamous Vigilance Committee, which hung eight men and scared off untold others. There were passageways known as Dead Man's Alley and Murderer's Corner, bars called

Hell's Kitchen and The Morgue. The core of the Barbary Coast was known as Devil's Acre, and a celebrated stretch of Kearny Street was called Battle Row. An 1879 editorial captures the Barbary Coast in all of its glory:

> *The petty thief, the house burglar, the tramp, the whoremonger, lewd women, cutthroats, murderers, all are found here. Dance halls and concert saloons, where bleary eyed men and faded women drink vile liquor, smoke offensive tobacco, engage in vulgar conduct, sing obscene songs and say and do everything to heap upon themselves more degradation, are numerous . . .licentiousness, debauchery, pollution, loathsome disease, insanity from dissipation, misery, poverty, wealth, profanity, blasphemy, and death, are there. And Hell, yawning to receive the putrid mess, is also there.*

But the lifeblood of the Barbary Coast was prostitution. Prices ranged from a quarter to $10, the highest price being fetched by any woman who either was, or convincingly pretended to be, a red-haired Jewess, thought to be the most passionate of all lovers. That money found its way to the highest levels of San Francisco government. The extent of the political and economic stake in the Barbary Coast was so great, in fact, that it was the first part of the City to rebuild after the Great Earthquake. Within three months of the cataclysm, a dozen whorehouses and as many saloons were back in full swing.

But the Earthquake also shook down a good deal of corruption in City Hall. By 1911, San Francisco decided that it no longer wanted to be the "Paris of America" and turned the political party of that promise out. By 1917, the Barbary Coast had been shut down and flushed out so completely that it is today difficult to find reminders of the area's infamous past. Much of it has been turned into the chic and darling Jackson Square district, a run of designer showrooms closed to the public. But if you look closely, you should be able to make out the outlines of some of the old saloons and dance halls, most of which seem to bridle at the unnatural infusion of style and circumstance to an area once so wholly given over to degeneracy. Here's where to look:

The Bella Union

Corner of Washington and Kearny Streets, near the Chinatown Holiday Inn. The Bella Union was easily the most famous and reputable of all the Barbary Coast saloons. The post-Earthquake version is now a movie theatre showing warmed-over American and Chinese movies.

Hippodrome Theatre

555 Pacific Street. Pacific Avenue, between Montgomery and Kearny Streets, was the heart of the Barbary Coast action and was often referred to as "Terrific Street." The Hippodrome was one of the mainstays of Pacific Avenue. The building is now a furniture showroom, but the distinctive (and scandalous in their time) reliefs on the front of the building remain.

St. Pierre

580 Pacific Avenue. Known as "Diana's" in its day, this is the only pre-Earthquake bar still standing. It's now a trendy restaurant.

Hotaling Warehouses

In Hotaling Alley, which runs from Washington to Jackson Streets, between Montgomery and Sansome. The Hotaling Distillery fueled the Barbary Coast. That the Hotaling warehouses made it through the Quake when a lot of more-reputable businesses fell prompted this popular ditty:

> *If, as they say, God spanked the town for being over-frisky,*
> *Why did He burn all the churches down and spare Hotaling's*
> *Whiskey?*

The block-long Hotaling Alley makes for a storied and charming walk. It runs off of the 500 block of Washington, across the street from the Transamerica Pyramid.

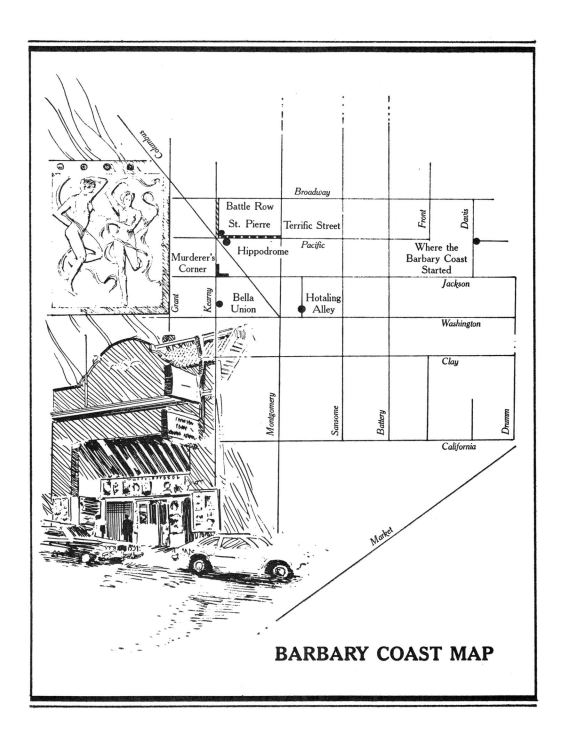

BARBARY COAST MAP

30 THE BEAT GENERATION

Like most everything else to happen in the shadow of the Golden Gate Bridge, the Beat Era came to pass not so much on account of San Franciscans as their city. The ruling elite of the Beats arrived in San Francisco from the World War II conscientious objector camps scattered across the West; from Denver, New York and Kansas; from Patterson, New Jersey, and Lowell, Massachusetts. They read poetry and blew jazz and chased the unwashed American Dream. They were called the Beat Generation, perhaps because of Jack Kerouac's cross-country vision of an on-going search for an endless love, or maybe just because of a highly attuned ear that picked up the rhythm of a decidedly different drummer. The Beat Generation has been called "the daddy of the swinging psychedelic generation." They're related, of course, but too much shouldn't be made of the connection. Both surfaced in the free-to-be climate of San Francisco, even shared some of the same faces—most notably Neal Cassady, Jack Kerouac's muse and Ken Kesey's fuse. But the hippies of the '60s participated in a social revolution. The Beats of the '50s, raw and angry, were more properly a literary movement.

Lawrence Ferlinghetti was one of the first to arrive in San Francisco. He hit town in 1951 and promptly set up shop in the City Lights Bookstore. Kerouac and Cassady were bouncing between the coasts at about the same time, and Kerouac captured their adventures in a burst of wild scat writing that he called "spontaneous prose." *On The Road* would go unappreciated and unpublished for years.

In 1953, Allen Ginsberg came out to see an old lover—the ubiquitous Neal Cassady—and stayed. Other artists began to queue up on the coast, until by 1955 it was plain to see that something special was happening in San Francisco. All doubt was removed 13 October 1955 at the Six Gallery, a small San Francisco art gallery. It was then that Ginsberg assembled "a remarkable collection of angels" for "wine, music, dancing girls, serious poetry, free satori." Kerouac would call it, "The night of the birth of the San Francisco Poetry Renaissance." Ginsberg himself stole the evening with a poem he had written just two weeks before in a peyote-amphetamine swirl. "Howl" blew the assembled minds that night, and the cover on the subterranean rebels. The San Francisco police hustled in to bust *Howl and Other Poems* when it was published in 1956, and the resulting trial rained publicity, people and problems down on the Beats and their North Beach haunt. Their reaction was to furrow even deeper into the cool underground, leaving behind a colorful montage of shops, coffeehouses and bookstores.

Following is a chronology of the short-lived Beat Era, and a map for a do-it-yourself archaeological dig. Dig it.

BEAT GENERATION

1944 Jack Kerouac, Allen Ginsberg and William Burroughs first assemble in New York City around Columbia University.

1946 Jack Kerouac meets Neal Cassady in New York City.

1947-50 Kerouac and Cassady make the cross-country sojourns that become the basis for *On The Road.*

1951 Kerouac writes *On The Road* in an inspired three-week sitting. The book is almost titled *The Beat Generation*, and defines "beat" as "short for beatitude . . . a spiritual quest for endless love." *On The Road* goes unpublished for years. The same year, Lawrence Ferlinghetti leaves New York for San Francisco "because it was the only place in the country where you could get decent wine cheap."

1953 Ferlinghetti opens City Lights Bookstore in North Beach. Ginsberg drops in on Neal Cassady in San Jose. Mrs. Cassady objects, so Cassady drives Ginsberg to San Francisco and leaves him.

1955 In November, Ginsberg organizes a poetry reading called "Six Poets at the Six Gallery." Ginsberg premieres "Howl" to the stoned and stunned audience. North Beach, like overnight, becomes a Scene.

1956 City Lights Books publishes *Howl and Other Poems* by Ginsberg. It is declared obscene by the San Francisco police, initiating a lengthy court battle and Media Event.

1957 *On The Road* is finally published and becomes a bestseller. *The New York Times* reviews it as "a major novel." Kerouac rejects a TV producer's offer to base a series on the weekly exploits of the book's two protagonists. The next season the producer places *Route 66* on TV, being the weekly exploits of two cross-country adventurers. It stars George Maharis, a ringer for Jack Kerouac.

San Francisco columnist Herb Caen coins the term "beatnik" to describe North Beach's growing community of shaggy artists. In September, *Life* magazine gives full-picture coverage to "Big Day for Bards at Bay," the *Howl* obscenity trial of Allen Ginsberg and City Lights publisher Lawrence Ferlinghetti. *Howl* is judged not obscene.

1958 National attention is now focused on North Beach and its crazy poets. *The San Francisco Examiner* reports with alarm that

CHRONOLOGY

"They've made their capital in North Beach—the 'Left Bank' of the West." *The Examiner* dutifully sends in a reporter to ferret out the truth. She reports that "They're the 'hipsters' and they're 'gone.' That's where they want to be . . . 'Far Out.' Some drink too much and some smoke 'pot' and others sexperiment. Some decorate a hunk of driftwood and try to sell it for 25 bucks so they can buy more beer. 'I just had a narrow escape, man. I almost found a job.' 'Look me in the eye.' 'Which I?' This is the chatter that fills their empty days."

In June, a young sax player dies when he falls off the roof of Eric Nord's Party Pad in North Beach. A few days later his girlfriend is found strangled. Bad vibes. In July, the ladies room at the Co-Existence Bagel Shop—a favorite of North Beach regulars—is blown up. In August, a number of Beats turn the tables on the tourists who prowl through North Beach in giant tour buses by renting a Gray Line bus for a tour of "Squaresville"—downtown San Francisco. J. Edgar Hoover turns literary critic the same month, reviewing Ferlinghetti's "Tentative Description of a Dinner Given to Promote the Impeachment of President Eisenhower" as a "nonsensical, difficult to understand dissertation . . . it appears Ferlinghetti may possibly be a mental case."

North Beach is beginning to overload now.

In September, the Alcoholic Beverages Commission declares "Beatnikland" a "problem area" and will issue no more liquor licenses. Eric Nord, always one of the most visible residents of North Beach, declares in court in November: "The Beat Generation is dead. I don't go to North Beach anymore." It's been only three years since the Scene was born at the Six Gallery.

1960   North Beach blows its main muses when The Place and the Co-Existence Bagel Shop close up.

1966   In March, *The San Francisco Examiner* gives front page coverage to the arrest of 25 "beatniks" who are led away chanting "LSD is reality." The address of the "beatnik pad" is 408 Ashbury Street, smack dab in the middle of the heretofore quiet Haight Ashbury district. Is the world ever in for a surprise.

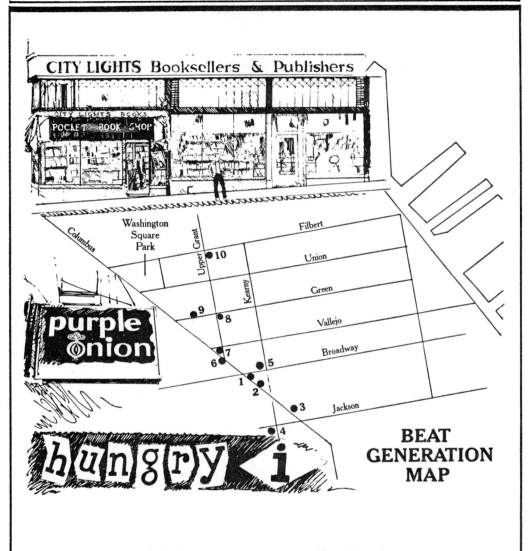

CITY LIGHTS Booksellers & Publishers

CITY LIGHTS BOOKS
POCKET BOOK SHOP

Columbus

Washington
Square
Park

Upper Grant

Filbert

● 10

Union

Kearny

Green

● 9

● 8

Vallejo

● 7

● 6

Broadway

● 5

● 1

● 2

● 3   Jackson

● 4

purple onion

hungry i

BEAT GENERATION MAP

1	City Lights Bookstore	6	Upper Grant Avenue
2	Vesuvio's	7	Caffe Trieste
3	Purple Onion	8	Co-Existence Bagel Shop
4	hungry i	9	The Cellar
5	Enrico's	10	The Place

WHERE ARE THEY NOW?

1. City Lights Bookstore 261 Columbus.
One of the high-water marks of the Beat Era.
Check out number 12 for the history and historical function of Lawrence Ferlinghetti's hip bookstore.

2. Vesuvio's 255 Columbus.
A sign out front says it all: "A gathering place of the people of North Beach since the days of 1949." Dylan Thomas regularly drank and passed out at Vesuvio's, as have most of the other lights of North Beach.

3. Purple Onion 140 Columbus.
Still at it after more than a quarter century. The Purple Onion discovered The Smothers Brothers (who recorded an album there), The Kingston Trio, Jim Nabors, Rod McKuen and Phyllis Diller. Now exists on the good will of tour groups.

4. hungry i 599 Jackson Street.
Helped launch Bill Cosby, Barbra Streisand, Mort Sahl and Professor Irwin Corey. The name of the club was later sold to a strip joint that has no other connection with the original.

5. Enrico's 504 Broadway.
Since 1958, Enrico Banducci, the King of North Beach, has watched the passing parade from his sidewalk cafe on Broadway. Enrico's is just another "must" in San Francisco.

6. Upper Grant Avenue.
During the height of the Beat Era, the stretch of Upper Grant Avenue between Columbus and Union was described as an "open-air, come-and-go mental hospital, three blocks long." It's still got the funk, if not the spunk.

7. Caffe Trieste 601 Vallejo (at Grant).
Then, as now, a popular coffeehouse for the North Beach irregulars. It's still 1955 in the Caffe Trieste.

8. Co-Existence Bagel Shop 1398 Grant Avenue (at Green Street).
The primordial coffeehouse of the North Beach literati. It closed in 1960.

9. The Cellar 576 Green Street (next to the Caffe Sporte).
A popular jazz club. Jack Kerouac wrote a poem about the bartender at The Cellar.

10. The Place 1546 Grant (near Filbert)
Kerouac described it in *The Dharma Bums* as "The favorite bar of the hepcats around The Beach." Every Monday night was "Blabbermouth Night," during which people were free to debate such subjects as "The superiority of the bagel as a contraceptive." It closed in 1960.

29 Russell Street
A small alleyway off Hyde Street, between Union and Green Streets. Jack Kerouac lived here with Neal and Carolyn Cassady during the winter of 1951-52. Kerouac and Cassady worked on the Southern Pacific Railroad. Kerouac stayed in the attic of the house and worked on *Visions of Neal*, *On The Road*, and *Doctor Sax*. Kerouac would later remember it as one of the best places he ever lived: "It rained every day, and I had wine, marijuana, and once in a while Neal's wife would sneak in."

Wentley Apartments 1214 Polk Street (between Bush and Sutter Streets).
Allen Ginsberg lived here for a time in the fall of 1955. It was here that he wrote "Howl" one long, stoned weekend. "Howl" was to become the centerpiece of the poetry reading Ginsberg organized two weeks later at the Six Gallery.

Six Gallery 3119 Fillmore Street (between Filbert and Greenwich Streets).
On 13 October 1955, Allen Ginsberg secured this tiny art gallery for "Six Poets at the Six Gallery," the electric moment that set The Movement in motion.

31 Haight Ashbury

In retrospect, the surest thing that can be said about the flowering of America in the '60s is that the Haight Ashbury was a very unlikely seed. The area—so named because of its principal intersection—had been a quaint, quiet and totally inconsequential San Francisco neighborhood. It survived the 1906 Earthquake intact, and over time had become a racially mixed black-and-white neighborhood full of rundown Victorians.

Then, around the beginning of 1966, a miracle of sorts occurred. There was a meaning to the moment that seems almost trite now. Suffice it to say, however, that there was no doubt on the street in 1966 that the small community of extra-sensory seekers was chosen.

One participant said at the time: "God has fingered that little block system between Baker and Stanyan Streets [on Haight Street]. And we spend all our time, verbally and non-verbally, trying to discover why." Another observed that "We thought there was going to be a breakthrough, and that it was imminent. I thought, 'There might be some room in this neighborhood where they've found a tunnel out.' "

The roots of the Haight Ashbury were the Acid Tests conducted by novelist Ken Kesey (*One Flew Over The Cuckoo's Nest*) and his Merry Pranksters. They started around Stanford University but eventually worked their way around the Bay Area, climaxing with the legendary Trips Festival in January of 1966. Just about all the sacramental trappings of psychedelia can be traced to the incredible three-day festival, as attested by this handbill from the event:

> *The general tone of things has moved on from the self-conscious happening to a more JUBILANT occasion where the audience PARTICIPATES because it's more fun to do so than not. Maybe this is the ROCK REVOLUTION. Audience dancing is an assumed part of all the shows, & the audience is invited to wear ECSTATIC DRESS & bring their own GADGETS (a.c. outlets will be provided.)*

It was Kesey who turned the Hell's Angels onto acid and brought them onto the Scene. And it was through Kesey that Augustus Owsley Stanley III, electric chemist, met the Grateful Dead. This prophetic pairing resulted in "Acid Rock," an indigenous San Francisco art form that combined music, lights and celebrants to approximate the psychedelic reverie—or heighten it, as the case might be. Acid rock was the crack in the cosmic egg that had been laid on an Ed Sullivan sound stage on 9 February 1964, when the Beatles appeared. It was no coincidence that the Beatles dropped acid, found God and produced their masterpiece—*Sgt. Pepper's Lonely Hearts Club Band*—all about the same time that several million hippies were invading San Francisco with flowers in their hair. George Harrison even bestowed Beatle blessings on the scene during a short visit to the Haight in 1967.

The importance of rock n roll in the new lifestyle was set forth in *The Oracle*, an underground paper in the Haight:

Some principles:

- *That rock is essentially head (or even psychedelic) music.*
- *That far from being degenerate or decadent, rock is a regenerative & revolutionary art, offering us our first real hope for the future (indeed, for the present) since August 6, 1945 . . .*
- *That rock is a way of life, international & verging in this decade on universal; and can't be stopped, retarded, put down, muted, modified or successfully controlled by typeheads, whose arguments don't apply & whose machinations don't mesh because they can't perceive (dig) what rock really is & does.*
- *That rock is a tribal phenomenon, immune to definition & other typographical operations, and constitutes what might be called a 20th Century magic.*

The magic could be found almost any night of the week in one of San Francisco's various rock temples: Bill Graham's Fillmore Auditorium (and later the Fillmore West), Winterland, Chet Helms' Avalon Ballroom.

Ultimately, however, the music sustained the moment long after the magic had died. It drew people to the Haight Ashbury for several years after the community had lost the ways or means to care for itself. The Summer of Love in 1967 nipped the flower in the bud. Dealers ("with the love grass in their hand") became pushers ("Goddamn, the pusher man") as hard drugs replaced psychedelics. By 1969 the Haight Ashbury was in the grips of a major heroin epidemic, which left its spirit broken and its streets ravaged.

Today the Haight Ashbury is on the roll again, but as a chic and increasingly gay district. You might have a hard time recognizing the old neighborhood now, but for this handy guide.

A SELECTED CHRONOLOGY OF THE LATE, GREAT HAIGHT ASHBURY

5 March 1965 Large quantities of Owsley Acid (the Cadillac of LSD) become available for the first time. A whole generation learns that their brain is no longer the boss.

13 August 1965 Folk singer Marty Balin opens a club called the Matrix and stocks it with his own group, the "sensational Jefferson Airplane." They would find acid and electricity at about the same time.

2 September 1965 On the night of the Beatles' San Francisco Cow Palace appearance, Ken Kesey hangs a sign on his south-of-San Francisco retreat that reads: "The Merry Pranksters Welcome the Beatles." The Beatles don't show, but one Augustus Owsley Stanley III does—aka "Owsley." Kesey, Owsley and acid would never be the same again.

5 September 1965 *San Francisco Examiner* writer Michael Fallon coins the term "hippie."

16 October 1965 Psychedelia's first rock concert. The Family Dog, a collection of loose people, stages "A Tribute to Dr. Strange" (a comic book character) in the unlikely setting of the Longshoreman's Hall on Fisherman's Wharf. The show stars the Jefferson Airplane and the Charlatans (with Dan Hicks) and features a light show.

6 November 1965 Bill Graham, then business manager of the San Francisco Mime Troupe, stages his first rock concert. It's a benefit, called Appeal I, to raise money for the Mime Troupe, busted for performing in the park without a permit.

10 December 1965 Bill Graham stages Appeal II, using a large hall he has secured in the black Fillmore section of San Francisco. Together, Bill Graham and the Fillmore Auditorium would make history.

3 January 1966 During January of 1966, the Haight Ashbury is born. Ron and Jay Thelin open the archetypal head shop in a small building on

Haight Street. The Psychedelic Shop serves as a catalyst for the growing "Hashbury" community, much as City Lights Bookstore had for the Beat Generation a decade before.

21-23 January 1966   Ken Kesey's Acid Tests lead ultimately to the biggest blowout of them all: the three day Trips Festival. Bill Graham is called in to handle the organization of the event, which is held in San Francisco's Longshoreman's Hall. Each of the three nights is different, but only the Saturday night show—featuring music by the Grateful Dead, a light show and strange behavior by the audience—is successful. Graham makes note of it all.

4 February 1966   Bill Graham puts on his first non-benefit show, patterned after the success of the Saturday night Trips Festival show. It's called "Bill Graham Presents the Jefferson Airplane with Sights and Sounds from the Trips Festival."

March 1966   The media begins to take note of the strange goings-on along the normally quiet Haight Street. *The San Francisco Examiner* gives front page coverage to the bust of 25 "beatniks" at 408 Ashbury Street, who are led away chanting "LSD is reality."

6 October 1966   Possession of LSD becomes a Federal offense.

October 1966   The community of minds continues to grow. The Diggers, mostly alumni of the Mime Troupe, sponsor free feeds daily in the Panhandle section of Golden Gate Park.

31 October 1966   Ken Kesey's Acid Test Graduation, originally scheduled for Winterland, is instead shunted off to an obscure warehouse on Harriet Street between Howard and Folsom Streets in the industrial South of Market district. Kesey says: "For a year we've been in the Garden of Eden. Acid opened the door to it . . . we've been going through that door and staying awhile and then going back out through that same door. But until we start going that far . . . and then going beyond . . . we're not going to get anywhere, we're not going to experience anything new. . . ." Very few people hear Kesey's message, and so are left to find out for themselves.

14 January 1967   Upwards of 20,000 people gather at the Polo Field in Golden Gate Park for a mass "Human Be-In—A Gathering of the Tribes." It is a community digging itself, awash in the moment and Owsley acid (supplied in the free turkey sandwiches passed out by the Diggers). The straight press is thrown into a tizzy trying to figure it out, but the *San Francisco Oracle* says simply: "The point was, we were there and it was happening."

9 March 1967   Anticipating some four million visitors to San Francisco during the Summer of Love, Bill Graham announces the Fillmore Auditorium will be open six nights a week.

5 April 1967   Gray Line Tours announces a "Hippie Hop," "The only foreign tour within the continental limits of the United States."

7 April 1967   Tom Donahue takes over KMPX, then a failing multilingual station, and turns it into a part-time progressive rock station. Donahue would later take the KMPX staff over to KSAN in the "Great Hippie Strike."

8 April 1967   The San Francisco Board of Supervisors resolves that hippies are unwelcome in San Francisco.

27 May 1967   "San Francisco (Be Sure To Wear Flowers)" by Scott MacKenzie enters the *Billboard* charts with the catchy refrain: "For those who come to San Francisco, summertime will be a love-in there/In the streets of San Francisco, gentle people with flowers in their hair." It would peak at #4 during the Summer of Love.

June 1967   *Sgt. Pepper's* by the Beatles is released.

16-18 June 1967   The Monterey Pop Festival is held down the California coast in Monterey. Performances by Janis Joplin and a variety of San Francisco bands panics the Los Angeles music industry into a mad raid on "The San Francisco Sound."

19 June 1967   Paul McCartney admits taking acid.

21 June 1967   A summer solstice party in Golden Gate Park officially begins the Summer of Love.

11 July 1967   Margot Fonteyn and Rudolf Nureyev, in town for a ballet performance, are busted with 16 others at a pot party at 42 Belvedere, in the Haight. An embarrassed San Francisco quickly drops charges.

3-6 August 1967   The drug scene begins to turn vicious, an omen of things to come. On the 3rd, John Kent Carter, a dealer more commonly called "Shob," is found dead with his arm severed at the elbow. He is known to have kept large amounts of money locked to his wrist. Three days later, William Thomas, alias "Superspade," is found in a sleeping bag dumped off a steep cliff in Marin County, a bullet in the base of his skull. He was last seen leaving to make a large drug deal.

7 August 1967   George and Patti Harrison, bedecked in heart-shaped specs, take a stroll down Haight Street, reporters in tow. They wander over

to Hippie Hill in Golden Gate Park where George strums a guitar, then walk back to their car and leave.

2 October 1967 The Dead House at 710 Ashbury Street is busted. The bust is given a feature photo spread in the premiere issue of a San Francisco-based hippie tabloid called *Rolling Stone*.

4 October 1967 The Psychedelic Shop closes. A sign out front reads: "Be Free" and "Nebraska Needs You More."

6 October 1967 The dream is over. A march through the Haight announces the "Death of Hippie, Loyal Son of Media," and the birth of "Free Man." Stereotypical hippie artifacts are loaded into a cardboard coffin and cremated. Haight Ashbury is dead, of overpopulation, overexposure and over-expectancy. It has been less than two years since the body of minds began to cohere at the Trips Festival.

WHERE ARE THEY NOW

Fillmore Auditorium Fillmore and Geary Streets. On 10 October 1965, Bill Graham staged a benefit for the Mime Troupe in an old auditorium in the black Fillmore section of San Francisco. Together, Graham and the Fillmore refined to high art the unique San Francisco phenomenon known as the dance/concert. Graham moved out of the original Fillmore on 4 July 1968 for the larger Fillmore West. The last night featured Creedence Clearwater Revival, Steppenwolf and It's A Beautiful Day.

Fillmore West Van Ness Avenue and Market Street. The Fillmore West carried the torch high for another three years. Graham would also take the "Fillmore" name back to his native New York, although he refused an offer to franchise the Fillmore across the country. In 1971, tired after five-and-one-half years with his shoulder to the boulder, Graham impulsively called it all off. The Fillmore West closed on 4 July 1971, with Santana, Creedence Clearwater Revial, Tower of Power and some high-powered San Francisco friends.

Winterland Post and Steiner Streets. Rock n roll's last temple. Graham shuffled his best draws off to Winterland, an old skating rink just two blocks from the original Fillmore. It was at Winterland that Peter Frampton recorded his chart-busting live album and that Graham staged the fabled "Last Waltz" for The Band and a few of their friends. (Lenny Bruce and the Sex Pistols also made their final appearances at Winterland.) When Graham lost his lease on Winterland, the dance/concert era in San Fran-cisco ended. The final show was on New Year's 1978, featuring the Blues Brothers and—who else—the Grateful Dead, making their 48th and final Winterland appearance.

Avalon Ballroom Van Ness Avenue and Sutter Street. The Avalon Ballroom evolved out of the jam sessions at 1090 Page Street by way of the Trips Festival. Chet Helms managed Big Brother and the Holding Company for a time, then became top Family Dog, which staged the first psychedelic dance/concerts. Helms' Avalon Ballroom and Graham's Fillmore Auditorium shared artists and efforts for awhile, then went head-to-head. Helms was "the spirit and soul of the Haight Ashbury," but not a terribly good businessman. The Avalon Ballroom is today the Regency II Theatre.

Matrix Club 3138 Fillmore Street. Marty Balin opened the Matrix in August of 1965 as a forum for his own group, the "sensational Jefferson Airplane." The neighbors protested when the Airplane went electric, so the group abandoned the club. It's now a bar called the Pierce Street Annex.

1090 Page Street Corner of Broderick Street. According to the people who used it, 1090 Page was "like the 'Y' of the Haight Ashbury." Back before the Fillmore and the Avalon there were the basement jam sessions at 1090 Page Street. Jerry Garcia jammed there, as did a group of players who called themselves "Big Brother and the Holding Company." The house was torn down in 1967.

112 Lyon Street Janis Joplin's residence in the Haight.

The Oracle 1371 Haight Street, upstairs. *The Oracle* was the most famous of the several San Francisco underground newspapers. It attempted to bring the psychedelic vision to print by breaking the page into a variety of geometric configurations and color codes, and by running stories without sequential hang ups.

Psalms Cafe Masonic and Haight Streets. Formerly the Drogstore Cafe. One of the last, true hippie hangouts on Haight Street. It's still 1967 in the Psalms.

The Dead House 710 Ashbury Street. Underwritten by Owsley, the Grateful Dead became the house band of the Haight and the first and leading proponent of Acid Rock. The Dead even kept a house and a high profile in the Haight. Their 1967 drug bust enlivened the first issue of *Rolling Stone*.

The Psychedelic Shop 1535 Haight Street. What it was. The prototype of the head shop, stocking all manner of supplies for the intrepid tripper. It opened in January of 1966 and closed in October of 1967, serving as a metaphor for the time of the Haight itself.

Pall Mall Lounge 1568 Haight Street. Bill Graham said: "For me, the Haight died the day I saw this sleezy, greasy little restaurant advertising 'Love Burgers.'" The Pall Mall doesn't serve "Love Burgers" anymore, but is still very greasy.

Tracy's Donuts 1569 Haight Street. A popular hangout because of its late hours.

The Blue Unicorn 1927 Hayes Street. The first coffeehouse in the Haight and the last stand of the bohemian refugees from North Beach.

636 Cole Street Between Haight and Waller Streets. Charles Manson's residence in the Haight.

Straight Theatre Haight and Cole Streets. Formerly the Haight Theatre, it became "The People's Ballroom." Denied a dance permit, it took to giving "dance lessons" with the likes of the Grateful Dead as "instructors." It has long since been closed and was finally torn down in 1979.

I-Thou Coffee Shop 1736 Haight Street. Opened in 1966 at the dawn of the Aquarian Age. Poetry readings encouraged patrons to be as beautiful as they were.

The Panhandle A block-wide tentacle that slithers out of Golden Gate Park between Fell and Oak Streets, parallel to Haight Street. The hippies appropriated it for daily Digger feeds and the occasional Grateful Dead concert.

Hippie Hill An otherwise nondescript hill near the tennis courts in Golden Gate Park and just a short walk from the Haight. It became a popular place to make music, friends, love, and connections, far from the prying eyes of the police.

Airplane House 2400 Fulton Street, on the fringe of the Haight and across from Golden Gate Park. The imposing black and gold mansion was picked up by the group in 1968, and has housed most of the members of the Jefferson Airplane/Starship at one time or another. Today it is used primarily as office space for the Starship, although it occasionally hosts the kind of blow-outs that were commonplace during the late '60s.

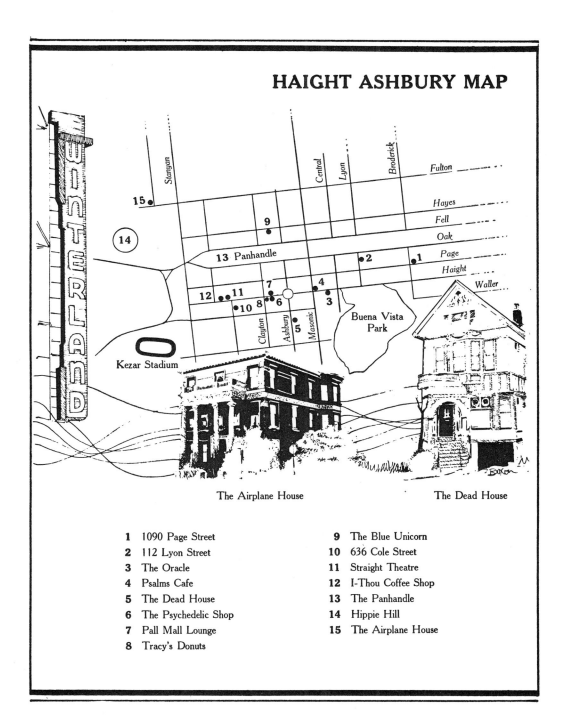

HAIGHT ASHBURY MAP

The Airplane House

The Dead House

1	1090 Page Street	9	The Blue Unicorn
2	112 Lyon Street	10	636 Cole Street
3	The Oracle	11	Straight Theatre
4	Psalms Cafe	12	I-Thou Coffee Shop
5	The Dead House	13	The Panhandle
6	The Psychedelic Shop	14	Hippie Hill
7	Pall Mall Lounge	15	The Airplane House
8	Tracy's Donuts		

32 DISCOVER YOUR ROOTS, CHILDREN OF THE SIXTIES

Couldn't make it to the Revolution? Thanks to a little hippie tabloid born in San Francisco you didn't need to. It came to you in convenient bimonthly installments from the front lines of the counter-culture. The unfolding drama was called *Rolling Stone*, after the group and after the titles of a Muddy Waters' song and Bob Dylan's first rock record. It was the offspring of an unnatural liaison between noted San Francisco jazz columnist Ralph J. Gleason and upstart Berkeley student Jann Wenner. It caused a lot of confusion when it first hit the streets in November of 1967 according to Ben Fong-Torres, Senior Editor of *Stone* and one of the first staff members aboard: "People couldn't tell what this 'underground hippie newspaper' was up to, whether it was a newspaper or a magazine, a trade or consumer publication, or whether it was about music, politics or just everything." Wenner himself admitted as much in the first issue: "You're probably wondering what we are trying to do. It's hard to say. . . ."

Wenner was being uncharacteristically modest. *Rolling Stone* had a very good grip on itself and the times that were a-changin' around it. While the rest of the media was only dimly aware of the gathering of minds that would erupt into a full-scale cultural revolution, *Rolling Stone* was dead square in the epicenter: San Francisco, 1967.

It couldn't have happened anywhere else. The reasons were patent, according to Fong-Torres. "There were a lot of symbols in San Francisco. It was because of the Haight Ashbury, because of the Panhandle, because of Ralph Gleason, because of the Fillmore and Bill Graham, Chet Helms and the Family Dog, Tom Donahue and KMPX that we got interested."

A funny thing happened along the way. *Rolling Stone* became respectable, even reputable. An award from the Columbia Graduate School of Journalism for *Stone*'s coverage of Charles Manson was a turning point for rock journalism. *Rolling Stone* scooped the world on the inside story of Patty Hearst's fugitive life. And Dr. Hunter S. Thompson's gonzo reports from the field helped alter a presidential election or two.

But the times they kept a-changin'. Ralph J. Gleason died. Wenner seemed to become obsessed with power and prestige. Blasting San

Francisco as a "sleepy backwater," he packed up his magazine and took it to New York in 1977. Fong-Torres explains that "It was very clear that what happened here has not happened again and probably should never happen again. What took place here in the '60s swept us up emotionally, musically, socially and politically. Compared to that we have nothing going on right now, regardless of how rich Bill Graham is."

No matter. The history of *Rolling Stone* and San Francisco are inexorably intertwined. San Francisco bore and nurtured the young magazine, lent it style, substance, and subject matter. If you'd like to see where *Rolling Stone* spent its formative years, head into the industrial "South of Market" area. Wenner cut a deal wth his first printer for the upstairs loft of a garish pink printing plant at 746 Brannan Street, which became the first *Rolling Stone* world headquarters. In 1970, the offices were moved to nearby 625 Third Street, where *Stone* still maintains a skeleton staff.

To find these places, head out Fourth Street from Market Street. To get to the fabled Pink Printing Plant, take a right off Fourth onto Brannan Street. You'll find 746 between Sixth and Seventh Streets. To get to the current offices, stay on Fourth to Townsend Street. Take a left onto Townsend, then another quick left onto Third Street. You'll see 625 about halfway up the block.

33 Lenny Bruce

If the name of Lenny Bruce doesn't immediately associate itself with San Francisco, it's because Lenny Bruce was more properly a product of the streets of New York and the neon netherworld of Los Angeles. It was in New York that a young Leonard Schneider bounced back and forth between the strict, responsible, upwardly-mobile home of his father and the reckless, temporary, star-struck world of his mother. It was in New York that Lenny Bruce won the Arthur Godfrey Talent Scout audition that convinced him that he, in fact, had some talent, and it was in New York that he first learned the *craft* of being a comic.

But it wasn't until he moved to Los Angeles that Lenny Bruce began to learn something of the *art* of being a comedian, night after smoky night in the bump and grind joints that would give him work. It was in L.A. that he began to connect with the jazz musicians whose language and lifestyle he would take as his own. And it was in L.A. that he built his contorted castle, The House on the Hill, where he would eventually retreat and die.

However, it was in San Francisco that Lenny Bruce developed his *style*. That style would take him past his contemporaries, beyond comedy, and outside of the realm of accepted taste in the late 1950's. It would make him a disposable hero to the upwardly hip and lead him to his inexorable end because, as he would say, "There's nothing sadder than an old hipster."

Following is a map and legend to the legend that Lenny Bruce helped create in San Francisco:

Ann's 440   440 Broadway. (Ann's 440 is now the Chi Chi Club, featuring comedy reviews.)

This is where Lenny Bruce got his first big break, smack dab in the middle of the Broadway street action. It was a lesbian joint, which is perhaps why owner Ann Dee felt an affinity with Lenny's scathing social satire. Ann Dee went down to Los Angeles looking for talent but came instead across Boots Malloy, the stage name of Lenny's mother, then posing as a comic. Boots turned Dee onto Lenny, who in turn turned Lenny onto San Francisco, who in turn turned San Francisco on its ear. Lenny came up in January of 1958 and stepped right into the middle of a major cultural overhaul. The beats were bopping up and down Broadway and all over North Beach. Poetry readings—the unique San Francisco hybrid of jazz and poetry—could be found almost any night of the week in the various coffeehouses that supported the scene. Mort Sahl held forth at the hungry i, serving notice that there was a comic consciousness beyond the rim shot and one-liner. The timing and the environment were perfect for Lenny. One of his most famous bits had a black hipster auditioning for a gig with Lawrence Welk, which brought down the legal wrath of the bubble king but also attracted the attention of Hugh Hefner and some Chicago nightclub owners. They swooped into San Francisco and picked up Lenny, and he remained a certified headliner the rest of his career.

Jazz Workshop 473 Broadway. (Jazz Workshop is now known as the Woffer Tavern/The Galaxie Night Club.)

On October 4, 1961, Lenny began his show by describing the clientele at Ann's 440 with a graphic, descriptive eleven letter expletive. He also explained, in a bit about semantics, that if you sterilize a toilet you no longer have dirty toilet jokes: ". . . obscenity is a human manifestation. The toilet has no central nervous system, no level of consciousness . . . it cannot be obscene." Shortly after his performance Lenny is busted for obscenity, the first in a series of such busts across the country that would eat up his time, money, and spirit. Lenny returned to do his second show, apologizing at the end that "I wasn't very funny tonight. Sometimes I'm not. I'm not a comedian. I'm Lenny Bruce." That fact, more than anything he said or did, would be the root of the troubles that would haunt him the rest of his life.

In the subsequent trial, Lenny is judged not obscene. His acquittal was a landmark decision, a career boost, and created a "safe" city he could return to again and again.

Swiss American Hotel   534 Broadway.

Then, as now, a seedy, run-down hotel in the heart of the Broadway action, the kind favored by Lenny Bruce. This was Lenny's second big break in San Francisco—literally. There are conflicting stories as to how Lenny Bruce actually came to be standing in the window of the Swiss American on March 29, 1965. One popular story has it that he was receiving oral gratification while leaning up against the window. A more authentic story has him jumping recklessly about the room in a drug haze. Whatever, Lenny tumbled out the window 25 feet to the parking lot below. Naked. Fortunately, he did a somersault in midair and actually landed on his feet, smashing both ankles and driving his bones up into his hips. He managed to keep enough presence of mind to curse the hospital attendants, who finally had to shut his mouth with adhesive tape.

Basin Street West   401 Broadway. (Basin Street West is currently the home of Enrico Banducci Presents the Entertainers, a showcase cabaret.)

The only filmed account of a Lenny Bruce concert was shot here in the spring of 1966. It's called simply *Lenny Bruce*, and shows a bloated caricature of Bruce lumbering through a mass of legal transcripts, as was his habit towards the end of his career.

Fillmore Auditorium   Fillmore and Geary Streets.

On June 24 and 25, 1966, Lenny Bruce played his final two dates at the hallowed Fillmore. Lenny could have hung on as an aging messiah to the budding Woodstock Generation, but he had no taste for it. He knew that he was used up and that his time was up: "There's nothing sadder than an old hipster." Lenny Bruce died just over a month later, on August 3, 1966.

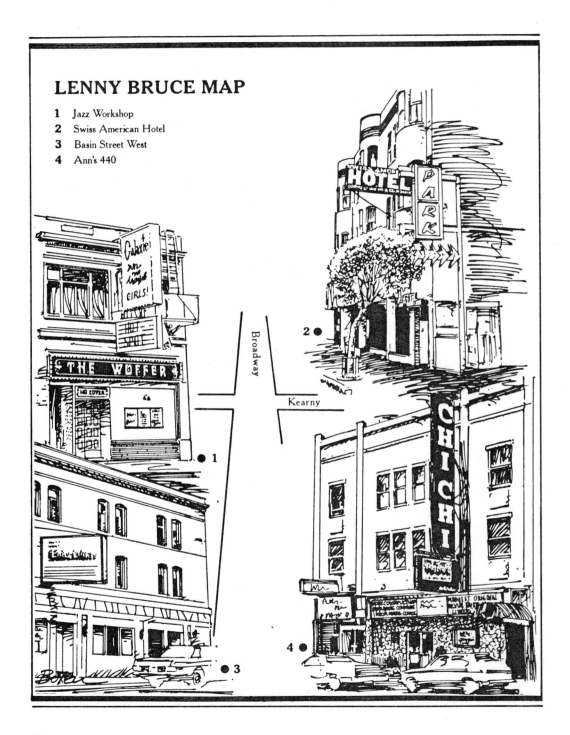

LENNY BRUCE MAP

1 Jazz Workshop
2 Swiss American Hotel
3 Basin Street West
4 Ann's 440

HISTORY

HISTORY

For all of its kinks and wrinkles, San Francisco is still a fairly young city. Although explorers had been combing the California coast for centuries, the San Francisco Bay wasn't even discovered until 1769. On July 4, 1776, the day the Declaration of Independence was signed a continent away, San Francisco was still but the distant dream of a couple of hearty settlers camped on a hill overlooking the bay. Neglected first by the Spanish and then by the Mexicans, the eventual settlement on the bay was forced to trade with its very enemies just to stave off starvation. By 1847, when the sleepy port town finally settled on San Francisco as its official name, its permanent population stood at only 900 people.

Then gold was discovered. From 1849 on, San Francisco has been a Commotion on the Ocean, more than making up for its former lack of presence. Although a good deal of San Francisco's colorful past was destroyed in the 1906 Earthquake and Fire, there's still enough around to fill up several museums. Here's where to find it, listed in order of approximate interest. Don't be put off by the number of places listed. San Francisco being the compact city that it is, you could easily see all the places mentioned here in one day. Budget two, however, if you want to savor the displays. If you're simply a glutton for punishment, fast forward to "Hansen's History on the Hoof," a walking tour through the heart of San Francisco's past.

A SELECTED CHRONOLOGY OF SAN FRANCISCO HISTORY

1542   Juan Rodrigus Cabrillo, Portugese explorer, sails blindly past the San Francisco Bay, but makes note of the Farallon Islands, a scant 32 miles off the coast.

1579   Sir Francis Drake, English explorer, sails past the Bay, even puts in a few miles north in what is today Drake's Bay.

1595   Sebastian Rodrigues Cermeno sails past as well, but puts in at Drake's Bay and christens it "La Bahia de San Francisco."

1769   One of the world's greatest natural harbors is finally discovered—by a land party looking for Monterey.

1775   Juan Manuel de Ayala pilots the first ship ever through the Golden Gate Strait. He appropriates "San Francisco Bay" from the ubiquitous harbor to the north and applies it to the marvelous body of water that stretches out before him. The settlement on the banks of the Bay would for years be called "Yerba Buena," however.

1776   As the thirteen colonies sign the Declaration of Independence a continent away, a party of hearty Mexican settlers is selecting the site for the Presidio (or fort) of San Francisco.

1821   Mexico gains independence from Spain and Yerba Buena falls under Mexican rule.

9 July 1846   War between Mexico and the U.S. Captain Montgomery sails into Yerba Buena and raises the American flag in Portsmouth Square.

30 January 1847   Yerba Buena aligns its name with that of its more famous harbor, and not a minute too soon. In less than a year, San Francisco would be the most famous port of call in the world.

May 1848   Sam Brannan, newspaper publisher, officially starts the gold rush when he walks through Portsmouth Square with a bottle of gold dust taken from the American River. Overnight, San Francisco drops from a population of 900 to 12, then swells to 35,000 by the end of 1849.

9 June 1851   San Francisco's infamous Vigilance Committee is formed to deal with the lawless lot that preys on San Francisco's weak defenses. A total of eight men are hung and scores more scared off.

1 August 1873   San Francisco's first cable car is piloted down Clay Street to Portsmouth Square by its inventor, Andrew Hallidie.

18 April 1906   The most notorious date in San Francisco history. At 5:13 a.m., The Big One strikes. By mid-morning, a number of small fires around the City begin to consolidate into the Great Fire that eventually destroys San Francisco.

1915   The Panama-Pacific Exposition celebrates the completion of the Panama Canal and San Francisco's return to robustness.

1917   The Barbary Coast is shut down.

2 August 1923   President Warren G. Harding dies in the Presidential Suite of the Palace Hotel, presumably from food poisoning.

1933   Alcatraz Island is turned over to the Department of Justice to be used as a maximum security penitentiary.

27 May 1937   Golden Gate Bridge opened.

26 June 1945   The charter creating the United Nations is signed at the War Memorial Opera House in San Francisco.

1957   The New York Giants become the San Francisco Giants.

11 August 1962   "I Left My Heart in San Francisco" by Tony Bennett enters the *Billboard* charts. It stays on the charts for twenty-one weeks.

October 1962   The Willie Mays-led Giants defeat the arch rival Dodgers in a dramatic three-game playoff for the pennant, but lose to the Yankees in the World Series.

1963   Alcatraz is closed.

19 June 1964   Carol Doda takes off her top in The Condor nightclub.

29 August 1966   The Beatles perform their last live concert ever in San Francisco's Candlestick Park.

34 THE OLD MINT

If you don't have a lot of time to spend history-hunting in San Francisco but would still like to get the gist of the City's lively past all the same, there's only one place you need to go: the Old Mint. For 63 years, the Old Mint was the San Francisco branch of the U.S. Mint (coins minted before 1937 bearing an "S" stamp were turned out of the Old Mint). Although it's in semi-retirement today, it's still used as the only special coin and medal mint in the U.S. system. The Old Mint acquired a name (The Granite Lady) and something of a reputation when it survived the 1906 Earthquake and Fire with only minor cosmetic damages. In 1971, the Old Mint was designated a National Historic Landmark, and in 1973 it was converted into today's interesting museum.

The Old Mint is stuffed with bits and pieces of San Francisco's rich history. Of particular interest is a recently discovered timber that was part of John Sutter's sawmill. (It was the discovery of a gold flake on the tail race of Sutter's sawmill that set off the 1849 California Gold Rush.) There's also a closely guarded pile of gold bars that was worth a million dollars when gold was worth $42 an ounce. You'll also find a restored stagecoach and fire engine, a collection of old phonographs, and a plausible explanation of how "U.S." came to mean "Uncle Sam." You can afford to miss a film (shown on the half hour) that recounts the story of "The Granite Lady," but not the guided tour that runs on the hour.

The Old Mint is at the corner of Mission and Fifth Streets, downtown. It's open Tues.-Sat. 10 a.m.-4 p.m. Phone 556-3630 or 556-6270. Free.

35 WELLS FARGO HISTORY ROOM

Few names stand for the Old Wild West like Wells Fargo. The now-giant banking corporation played a legitimate role in hauling civilization out of the sitting rooms of the East and depositing it in the woolly West. It's therefore only natural that Wells Fargo would gather a few historical artifacts into a museum. Happily, the Wells Fargo Bank History Room turns out to be authentic, well-documented and graciously unpatronizing. The biggest draw is an actual Wells Fargo stagecoach, which will quickly dispel any romanticized notion you have of life in the Old West. A checklist for passengers warns against drinking in cold weather "because you will freeze twice as quickly when under its influence"; advises against pointing out the specific locations of murders, "especially if there are women passengers"; and forewarns passengers: "Don't imagine for a moment that you are going on a picnic. Expect annoyances, discomfort, and some hardship."

The Wells Fargo Bank History Room is located in the Wells Fargo World Headquarters, 420 Montgomery Street (corner of California Street) in the Financial District. Open Mon.-Fri. 10 a.m.-3 p.m. Phone 396-2649. Free.

36 Fort Point

If you can see the Golden Gate Bridge, then you can probably see Fort Point, tucked away under the support tower of the bridge on the San Francisco side. Fort Point is called the "Silent Sentinel of History," and for good reason. In three different incarnations, under two different flags and through four different wars, Fort Point has never fired a single shot in defense of its country. Lucky thing, too, because Fort Point was the last brick fort ever built in the U.S. — and the only one west of the Mississippi. Brick was rendered obsolete in one fell blow when South Carolina's Fort Sumter was fired on at the beginning of the Civil War.

In this century, Fort Point was used as a base of operations during the construction of the Golden Gate Bridge. It was later manned during World War II by soldiers tending a submarine net stretched across the entrance to the San Francisco Bay. But that's about it for the little fort that could.

Today, Fort Point is open to interesting self and guided tours. Although it's visible under the Golden Gate Bridge, getting to it is a little tricky. Phone 556-1693 for instructions. It's open seven days a week, 10 a.m.-5 p.m. Tours are given weekdays every hour on the hour, weekends every half hour. Free. Even on the warmest days, Fort Point is quite chilly, so bring along a sweater or a jacket.

37 Mission Dolores

If you really start digging into San Francisco's past, you can't go back any further than the Mission Dolores in the Mission District. The humble adobe church is the very root of San Francisco, the oldest existing structure in the area. The original Mission was built by the Spaniards in 1776 as the sixth in a chain of 21 California missions, ostensibly to bring religion to the Indians, but in fact to lay claim to the new territory—which is why the Presidio (or "fort") of San Francisco went up at the same time.

The most amazing thing about the Mission Dolores is that it's still standing after all these years. It held up even during the Earthquake (a more modern church next to it crumpled), and was miraculously spared when the Fire burned out just one block away. The attached museum is surprisingly lackluster, but an adjacent cemetery—one of only two cemeteries in all of San Francisco—carries a star-studded historical cast, including James Casey and Charles Cora, the last two victims of San Francisco's infamous Vigilance Committee.

The Mission Dolores provides good reason to take BART into the colorful Mission District. If you allow yourself time for a meal while there, you'll let yourself in on some of the best — and most inexpensive — eating in San Francisco. The Mission Dolores is at Dolores and 16th Streets (just three blocks from BART's 16th Street Mission stop). It's open seven days a week, 9 a.m.-4:30 p.m. (shorter hours in the winter). Phone 621-8203. Donation requested.

38 Society of California Pioneers Museum

More San Francisco history, though not in nearly as interesting a setting as the Old Mint and without the unifying theme of the Wells Fargo Museum. The genuine show stopper here is the bell that called the infamous San Francisco Vigilance Committee to law and order. There's also a replica of the famous first flake taken off of John Sutter's sawmill that started the mad rush to San Francisco. Recommended if you're intent on digging into San Francisco, but only as a fifth recourse.

The Society of California Pioneers Museum is at 456 McAllister Street, near City Hall. It's open Mon.-Fri. 10 a.m.-4 p.m. Phone 861-5278. Free.

39 PRESIDIO ARMY MUSEUM

Despite the fact that they're never been challenged for San Francisco, the U.S. Army has nonetheless run up a substantial history over two centuries of occupation. The military has at one time or another held claims to each of the four islands in the San Francisco Bay (Angel, Treasure and Yerba Buena Islands, and Alcatraz) and over 4500 acres on either side of the Golden Gate Bridge. In 1974, all that history was gathered up and put on display in the Presidio Army Museum (formerly an Army hospital and one of the first permanent structures in San Francisco). For military buffs, the museum is a find. For the rest of us, it has its moments. Of special interest are a collection of World War II propaganda posters and Thomas Edison's

1897 plan to defend San Francisco by extending giant electrical cables across the bay and luring an unsuspecting enemy over them: "All would be stretched dead in the attempt to enter. This would be a strategem far surpassing in cunning and effectiveness the famous wooden dodge of the ancient Greeks in their siege of Troy." For better or worse, history will never know.

The Presidio Army Museum is on the Presidio Army Base, near the San Francisco side of the Golden Gate Bridge. Open Tues.-Sun. 10 a.m.-4 p.m. Phone 561-4115. Free.

40 TEN PLACES WHERE YOU CAN SEE PICTURES OF THE GREAT SHAKE AND BAKE

First things first: although San Francisco averages some twenty to thirty shakers a year, when speaking of such things, there is only one earthquake—*The* Great Earthquake of 1906.

It hit at 5:13 on the morning of 18 April 1906 and was felt in two violent shocks lasting a total of 65 seconds. The earth shifted an average of 10 feet horizontally along the San Andreas Fault, registering an estimated 8.3 on the Richter Scale. That's powerful enough to overturn heavy furniture and shake down poorly designed buildings. It remains to this day the most violent quake ever to hit the continental United States. One survivor likened it to "a terrier shaking a rat." Contrary to popular legend, however, San Francisco did withstand the Earthquake fairly well, primarily because the San Andreas Fault passes out to sea just before it hits San Francisco.

San Francisco fared much worse in the ensuing fires that sprang up within minutes of the Quake. Whatever plans the City had for handling a major conflagration were buried in the rubble of the main fire house with San Francisco's fire chief. San Francisco was defenseless before the Blaze. Had it not been for a fortuitous shift of wind, the Fire probably would have raged until there was no more San Francisco to ravage. Even at that, the Fire burned for three days. It destroyed four-and-one-half square miles of prime San Francisco, an area half again as large as that destroyed in the Chicago fire started by Mrs. O'Leary's famous cow.

The Great Earthquake and Fire did $500 million worth of damage (in 1906 dollars) by destroying 490 square blocks and 28,000 buildings. The death toll was 674, including 315 who were found, 352 who weren't and seven looters who were shot on sight.

However, words and statistics are hardly up to the job of portraying the extent of the destruction. Only in photographs is it possible to really sense the full force of the holocaust. Fortunately, several places around San Francisco have good collections. For starters, here are 10 that are easy to get to or are on your way to someplace else, all free:

Old Mint Fifth and Mission Streets, downtown 556-3630
Cable Car Museum 1201 Mason Street (at Washington) 474-1887
Fireman's Pioneer Museum 655 Presidio Avenue (at Pine Street)
Tommy's Joynt Geary Street at Van Ness Avenue 775-4216
North Beach Museum 1435 Stockton Street (in the Eureka Federal Savings Building)
Presidio Army Museum Presidio Army Base 561-4115
Society of California Pioneers Museum 456 McAllister Street (across from City Hall) 861-5278
Earthquake McGoon's 128 Embarcadero 986-1433
Hoffman's Grill 619 Market Street, downtown 421-1467
Mission Dolores 16th and Dolores Streets, Mission District 621-8203

By the way, if you're worried about another earthquake hitting San Francisco, you have every right to be. In the words of one expert, "The further you are from the last big earthquake the nearer you are to the next." The good news is that the average time between big quakes is about 100 years, which gives us roughly till the year 2006. Relax and stay awhile.

41 The World's Largest Swimming Pools

If you take an ocean drive out along San Francisco's Great Highway, you'll come across a couple of inadvertent museums. The ruins of the once-elegant Sutro Baths and the remains of the enormous Fleishhacker Pool are eloquent reminders of the grandeur that was San Francisco. The swimming pools (and that's putting it mildly) were built to order for San Francisco at the beginning of the century: extravagant, optimistic and totally out-of-synch with reality. The Sutro Baths were the most lavish pools that San Francisco—or any city—has ever seen. Built in 1896 on the rocks just below the Cliff House on the Pacific edge of the City, the Sutro Baths was an incredible glass hulk, "the world's largest glass building." At high tide, fresh ocean water circulated through seven pools, arranged at 10-degree intervals from ice cold to 80 degrees warm. To swim was just to begin, however. There were also several restaurants, a museum, ping pong tables and an assortment of trapezes, swings and slides. In all, the Sutro Baths was built to accommodate 10,000 swimmers and some 15,000 spectators.

Fleishhacker Pool, adjacent to the zoo on the Great Highway, also tried to take advantage of the plentiful supply of ocean water. It failed to take into account the double-whammy of wind and fog. When Fleishhacker was opened in 1925, it comfortably laid claim to being the largest swimming pool in the world. At 1000 feet, it's longer than three football fields laid end to end. It took good eyesight just to see from one end to the other.

Unfortunately, both pools were designed for an immobile population. When the two bridges on the bay were opened in the '30s, San Franciscans headed for the warmer natural beaches up and down the California coast. Without a crowd, Sutro Baths became a lonely old edifice. It was closed in 1952 and burned to its foundations in a 1966 fire. The skeleton of the pools can still be seen from the Cliff House.

The wind-racked Fleishhacker Pool made it until 1971. Then in 1976, it was mercifully voted under by the people of San Francisco. The zoo will eventually expand into the area now occupied by the pool, so you have to look quick if you want to see it.

42 HANSEN'S HISTORY ON THE HOOF

If you haven't had enough history yet, then you may just be foolish enough to attempt "Hansen's History on the Hoof," a two-hour walking tour through the heart of San Francisco's past. And present, too, since the two live on the same streets—of necessity, San Francisco being so cramped that it's never had the luxury of outgrowing any part of town.

"Hansen's History on the Hoof" is also a pleasant, relatively painless procession through downtown San Francisco, the Financial District and Chinatown. If you're ready, pick a nice day, pack a firm resolve and begin with a single step.

Hansen's History on the Hoof" starts at Hallidie Plaza, the area around the Powell Street cable car turnaround on Market Street. Near the escalator to BART you'll find a (1) granite block fitted with an actual cable car grip and a grateful inscription honoring Andrew Hallidie, inventor of the cable car. Head three blocks north up Powell Street to Union Square. A (2) commemorative marker in the southwest corner of the park points out that Union Square was the center of pioneer San Francisco.

Three blocks further up Powell Street, you'll come to Bush Street. (For this ascent, it's perfectly all right to flag down a passing cable car.) The 600 block of Bush is one of the most interesting in the City. Robert Louis Stevenson lived at (3) 608 Bush during the winter of 1879/80. A plaque out front notes that he "wrote essays, poems, autobiography and fiction" while there. Just a few steps from 608 is an alley called Monroe Street. Dashiell Hammet wrote *The Maltese Falcon* at (4) 20 Monroe Street. Across Bush Street is another small alleyway called Burritt Street, where (5) "Miles Archer, partner of Sam Spade, was done in by Brigid O'Shaughnessy" in *The Maltese Falcon*, as is noted on a brass marker.

Continuing down Bush Street to Montgomery, you'll pass the site of the (6) California Theatre at 444 Bush Street (now the Telephone Building), one of the most sumptuous of its day. If you take a left onto Montgomery Street from Bush (fortunately, everything is on flat ground from here on out), you'll be walking along San Francisco's original waterfront, so noted on the (7) California First Bank Building on California between Sansome and Battery.

Montgomery Street, the first principal artery of San Francisco, is loaded with historical plaques. On Montgomery between Sacramento and Clay Streets is a marker noting the (8) California headquarters of the British-chartered Hudson Bay Company, built in 1841 when California was still under Mexican rule. England never pressed her advantage. Just up the street is a small, alley-like byway called Commercial Street. One of San Francisco's first newspapers, (9) *The Evening Bulletin*, was located at the corner of Montgomery and Commercial Streets. In 1856, publisher James King of William (that was his name) printed some dirt about James Casey, prompting the latter to shoot and kill King of William.

San Francisco was so outraged that a second Vigilance Committee was born and empowered to arrest and hang Casey. The deed was done from (10) Fort Gunnybags, committee headquarters. The site is now a parking lot on Sacramento Street, between Front and Davis Streets. A plaque marks the spot.

At (11) 608 Commercial Street is a one-story building that was the first site of the U.S. Branch Mint in San Francisco. It used to be three stories, but the top two were dynamited so the Great Fire would pass over it. Back on Montgomery Street, at the corner of Merchant Street, is the site of the (12) western terminus of the very first run of the Pony Express. The year was 1860.

At this point you're standing across the street from the Transamerica Pyramid, located on one of the most famous pieces of real estate in San Francisco. Inside the pyramid, a plaque notes that it is built on the site of the old (13) Montgomery Block, the first fireproof building in San Francisco, and the place where James King of William died after being shot just up the street. It was here also that Mark Twain met Tom Sawyer, and that Sun Yat-sen wrote the 1911 Chinese Constitution. The lobby restaurant, called The Bank Exchange, bears a reminder of the legendary (14) Pisco Punch, a drink that passed onto Heaven with its creator.

The last stop on the tour is at Portsmouth Square, the "cradle of San Francisco." From the Transamerica Pyramid, take Washington Street one block west to Kearny Street. Portsmouth Square is a veritable primer in San Francisco history. Various inscriptions about the park note that it was here that (15) the American flag was first raised over San Francisco back in 1846, and that it was here also that (16) the discovery of gold at Sutter's Mill was first announced to the world in 1848. A rock covered with bird droppings also marks the spot where the (17) world's first cable car ended its historic first run on 1 August 1873—successfully. Robert Louis Stevenson, who spent a lot of time in the park, is remembered by (18) a sailing ship memorial. Finally, look for one of the many (19) benches scattered about the park. These benches don't stand for anything. You shouldn't, either. Sit. You've earned the rest.

HANSEN'S HISTORY ON THE HOOF MAP

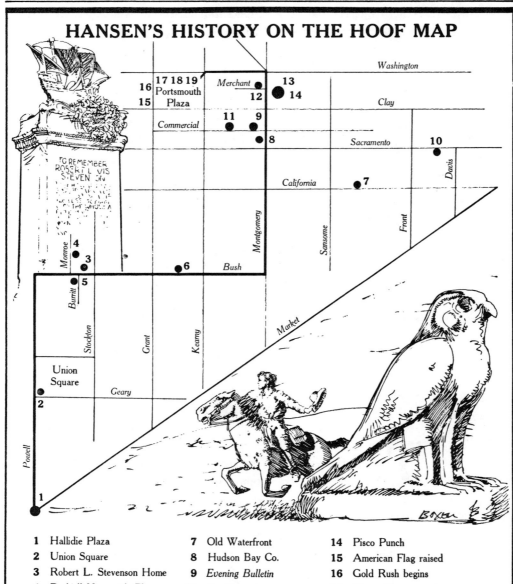

1 Hallidie Plaza	**7** Old Waterfront	**14** Pisco Punch
2 Union Square	**8** Hudson Bay Co.	**15** American Flag raised
3 Robert L. Stevenson Home	**9** *Evening Bulletin*	**16** Gold Rush begins
4 Dashiell Hammett's Place	**10** Fort Gunnybags	**17** First cable car terminus
5 Miles Archer done in here	**11** U.S. Branch Mint	**18** Robert L. Stevenson Memorial
6 California Theater	**12** Pony Express terminus	**19** Benches
	13 Montgomery Block	

CULTURE

43 San Francisco Museum of Modern Art

The "Modern" is a recent addition to the museum's title, serving to identify the museum's purpose and to lay claim to the distinction of being the only museum in the West devoted exclusively to twentieth century art. Its permanent collection includes works by Dali, Ernst, Matisse, Picasso, and Monet. The San Francisco Museum of Modern Art also takes a bow for being one of the first museums in the country to recognize film as a serious art form.

The often imaginative showings are housed in the confines of the War Memorial Building at Van Ness Avenue and McAllister. The galleries are open Tue., Wed. and Fri. from 10 a.m. to 6 p.m.; Thur. till 10 p.m.; and Sat.-Sun. 10 a.m.-5 p.m. A tour is offered Tue.-Sun. at 1:15 p.m. Phone 863-8800. Admission. A first floor bookstore is a particular delight, and is a good place to browse if you're looking for an unusual gift.

44 The M.H. deYoung Memorial and Asian Art Museums

The M.H. deYoung Museum and the Asian Art Museum are two quite distinct and distinguished collections of art housed in the same building on the Music Concourse in Golden Gate Park. The titular deYoung was the founder and original publisher of *The San Francisco Chronicle*. He convinced San Francisco to show off Golden Gate Park in the fruitful California Midwinter Fair of 1894/95, which left the nucleus of today's "Heart of the Park." The pay-off to deYoung was that the City gathered up some of the art displayed at the fair, hung it in a leftover building and christened it the deYoung Museum. The present building was built later, with one of the wings subsequently given over to a bequethal of Oriental treasures from Avery Brundage (the same former president of the International Olympic Committee).

The European Collection in the central building of the deYoung Museum starts in Ancient Egypt, advances chronologically through the Renaissance, into the Age of Rembrandt and ends up with American art. In the East Wing is a less staid and ultimately more interesting arrangement of primitive art and artifacts from tribal societies, including African, American and South American Indians and Eskimos. The Brundage Collection in the West Wing takes in some 4000 years of Chinese and Asian culture. It will take you only slightly less time to do it justice.

The deYoung Museum is in Golden Gate Park. It's open seven days a week, 10 a.m.-5 p.m. Free daily tours of the various wings are offered, all starting between 1 and 2 p.m. Phone 752-5561. Admission (which allows you same-day entrance to the California Palace of the Legion of Honor). Free the first day of each month.

45 *California Palace of the Legion of Honor*

A beautiful building showcases this collection of French art and culture from the fourteenth through the nineteenth centuries. The emphasis is on the works of the sculptor Rodin, whose "Thinker" cogitates just outside the entrance. The museum itself is stunning. It's modeled after the French Legion of Honor on the banks of the Seine. No less impressive, however, is the setting for the American copy, overlooking the Pacific and the Golden Gate Bridge. Even if the French art doesn't get you, the breathtaking view will.

To get to the California Palace of the Legion of Honor, take Geary Boulevard west, and then take a right on 34th Avenue. It's open seven days a week, 10 a.m.-5 p.m. A tour is offered every day at 2 p.m. Phone 558-2881. Admission (which allows you same-day entrance to the deYoung Museum in Golden Gate Park). Free the first day of each month.

46 Palace of Fine Arts

If you enter San Francisco from the Golden Gate Bridge, you'll see a beautiful side of the City, fronted by a stylish domed building. The building is the Palace of Fine Arts, an elegant Roman ruin surrendering peacefully to time by the banks of a quiet lagoon.

What?

The Palace of Fine Arts is a survivor from the 1915 Panama-Pacific Exhibition, a world's fair commemorating the completion of the Panama Canal. There were ten such lavish buildings arranged around a rectangular court, all representing, "the mortality of grandeur and the vanity of human wishes." The buildings were made only of "staff," however, a temporary substance that can be fashioned to look like stone or marble. After the fair was over, all of the buildings were torn down—all, that is, except for the Palace of Fine Arts, which was allowed to stand . . . and stand. By 1959, it was in a serious state of rot. Enter a wealthy and sentimental benefactor, offering $2 million to rebuild the Palace of Fine Arts if the City would respond in kind. In an act of public largess that would be unheard of in these post-Proposition 13 times, San Francisco agreed. The old Palace was torn down and replaced with the new Palace, this time built to last.

Besides grounds for a pleasant walk, the Palace of Fine Arts houses the Exploratorium (see #17) and the infrequently used Palace of Fine Arts Theatre, site of the second presidential debate in 1976 between Jimmy Carter and Gerald Ford.

The Palace of Fine Arts is in the Marina District, near the entrance to the Golden Gate Bridge.

47 THE CALIFORNIA ACADEMY OF SCIENCES

The California Academy of Sciences in Golden Gate Park is a labyrinth of six building additions arranged around an open-air courtyard. You'll probably run out of time before you do exhibits, although most of the exhibits tend to be routine for natural science museums. A couple of the exceptions are a live, two-headed snake housed in the reptile section of the Steinhart Aquarium, and Laserium, a rock n roll laser show that tends to boggle.

The Academy of Sciences is a great way to spend a rainy day in San Francisco, but absolutely nowhere if the sun is shining. It's in Golden Gate Park, near the main concourse. It's open seven days a week, 10 a.m.-9 p.m. (shorter hours in the winter). Phone 752-8268. Admission. The Laserium keeps separate hours, so call ahead for showtimes at the same phone number.

FISHERMAN'S WHARF

Fisherman's Wharf

Fisherman's Wharf, like most everything else in San Francisco, was conceived in sin. The very first dock on the Wharf was put up back in 1854 by one "Honest" Henry Meiggs, in an attempt to drive up the value of his nearby North Beach property. When Meiggs' Wharf collapsed, San Francisco discovered too late that the dock had been financed with forged city warrants. Ol' "Honest" Henry took a fast boat to Peru, leaving San Francisco to take the fall.

The area didn't become known as Fisherman's Wharf until after the Italians arrived on the scene in the 1870s. The Italians quickly took over the Wharf, aided by some discriminatory legislation that effectively kept the Chinese out of the water. As their fishing trade grew, a few of the industrious families took to cooking a portion of their day's catch right out on the docks in big crab pots. At first, only the returning fishermen were privy to these daily feeds, but in time some curious natives began chancing the trip into the rough Wharf district. These sidewalk kitchens eventually gave way to small family restaurants. (Fisherman's Grotto, the first, opened in 1936.) In short time, word spread about the excellent seafood restaurants down on Fisherman's Wharf.

But Fisherman's Wharf didn't begin to evolve into the mega-attraction it is today until shortly after World War II. Old-timers will tell you that Joe DiMaggio hastened the evolution more than anyone or anything, simply by being a highly visible and popular product of the Wharf sandlots. But even as late as the early '50s, Fisherman's Wharf was still little more than a dilapidated warehouse district. It was then that the City decided to capitalize on the Wharf's growing reputation. An abandoned WPA building was converted into a striking Maritime Museum (it was already conveniently shaped like a ship) and surrounded by a park. The City then gathered up five ships that

had worked the San Francisco Bay and anchored them off the Wharf. A planned antique car museum never came off.

In 1958, Cost Plus, an import shop, tested the retail waters on Fisherman's Wharf and found them very, very good. In 1964, the old Ghirardelli Chocolate Factory was converted into a striking shopping area, followed quickly by The Cannery, which was hollowed out of an old Del Monte peach-packing plant. The most recent addition to the busy area came in 1978 when an abandoned pier at the east end of the Wharf action was fitted with an array of shops and restaurants and christened Pier 39.

You don't need any help finding things to do along Fisherman's Wharf, but here are a few ideas anyway. The only way to do the Wharf is by foot. The best and most convenient way to get there is by cable car. Also, check out number 22, so you'll understand a bit about the mysterious sourdough process when you pause at the Boudin Bakery picture window on Jefferson Street; and number 11 so you'll be tempted to join the perpetual crowd at the Buena Vista Cafe at Hyde and Beach Streets, near the Hyde Street cable car turnaround.

48 Discover the Real Fisherman's Wharf

The transformation of the once-shaggy stretch of waterfront warehouses into today's Fisherman's Wharf has been complete. So much so, in fact, that the colorful fishing boats that bob along the Wharf seem almost to be a charming afterthought of an enterprising developer. The fishermen who lent their name have almost been crowded off the Wharf and are all but impossible to find—unless, of course, you know where to look. Which, it turns out, you do, thanks to another "Hansen's History on the Hoof," this time through the *real* Fisherman's Wharf.

You have to get up pretty early to catch the fishermen. They're out on their boats by about 4 a.m., warming up to the day ahead in animated conversation. You'll find them along the (1) docks on Jefferson Street, between Taylor and Jones Streets, across from DiMaggio's Restaurant.

If you turn down a small alleyway next to Castignola's Restaurant on Jefferson Street, you'll enter (2) Fish Alley. Walk down Fish Alley to Scoma's Restaurant, where you'll be able to see the fish-packing plants, the real business of Fisherman's Wharf. This is where the returning fishing boats dump off their daily catch. The fish are then put on ice and packed off to restaurants around the Wharf and the country.

Your last stop on the real Wharf is a restaurant that has for years taken the chill off the bones of fishermen and wharf-watchers alike. The grand (3) Eagle Cafe now sits on an unlikely second floor perch in Pier 39. That's because it got bumped off its original site during construction of the complex. No matter. The Eagle Cafe still serves the most honest cup of coffee on the Wharf. It's the best place to end your early-morning odyssey into the real Wharf and a great way to start your day. The venerable Eagle opens at 6 a.m., seven days a week. Phone 433-3689.

49 SHIVER YOUR TIMBERS

The San Francisco Maritime Museum is actually a three-parter spread along the entire length of Fisherman's Wharf. The Maritime Museum is headquartered in Aquatic Park (across Beach Street from Ghirardelli Square) in a building that is designed, coincidentally, to look "like a huge ship at its dock." The building was actually built during the Depression and was intended as a bath house for nearby

Aquatic Beach. (That no more than a handful of the proposed 5000 daily bathers ever showed up to swim in the icy waters of the bay shows that although people may have been depressed, they certainly weren't crazy.) The museum took over the building in 1951, filling it with a variety of model ships, figureheads, anchors, and other nautical artifacts.

The more interesting displays are anchored in the bay. The Maritime State Historic Park at the foot of Hyde Street is a living museum. It features five of the actual workhorse vessels that lugged and tugged men, machines and material in and out of the bay during the golden age of San Francisco shipping. The routine of the various shipboard existences has been faithfully recreated, giving a true sense of the severe rigors and scant pleasures of workaday sea life.

The star of the harbor is *The Balclutha*, a majestic square rigger that made some 17 trips "Around the Horn" between 1886 and 1904. She was twice washed up and left for dead, and spent another 20 years in Hollywood as an anonymous movie backdrop. In 1954, the San Francisco Maritime Museum borrowed enough money to retrieve the broken shell of a ship. *The Balclutha* was then refloated and refitted in something of a miracle. Eighteen Bay Area labor unions donated their time and talent to restore *The Balclutha* for use as a floating museum to which end she's been marvelously stocked with a variety of sailing memorabilia.

About the only problem with the excellent Maritime Museum is that there's too much of it. If you try to see it all in one day you'll be so steeped in sea lore you won't know if you're heading fore or aft. Spread it out over two days if you have the time, or be selective in this order: (1) *The Balclutha*; (2) Maritime State Historic Park; and (3) Maritime Museum.

The main museum of the San Francisco Maritime Museum is in Aquatic Park, across Beach Street from Ghirardelli Square. It's open seven days a week, 10 a.m.-5 p.m. Phone 556-8177. The five ships of the Maritime State Historic Park are anchored at the foot of

Hyde Street, just one block from the Hyde Street cable car turn-around. It's open seven days a week, 10 a.m.-5 p.m. Phone 556-6435. *The Balclutha* is anchored at Pier 43. You won't have any trouble spotting her giant masts on the Wharf skyline. Open seven days a week, 9 a.m.-10:30 p.m. Phone 982-1886. Each part of the Maritime Museum has a separate admission.

50 CATCH A FISH, SPORT

Even if you've never baited anything more than a sucker, you can still become the daring deep-sea fisherman of your dreams. The two agencies listed below will make all the necessary arrangements and have you out on the ocean by tomorrow. The cost for a day of fishing is around $30, which includes a rod, bait and tackle, as well as a fishing license, good for three days. The boats leave at about 6 a.m. and return at 3 p.m. daily, weather permitting. All you have to do is pack a lunch and bundle up against the morning chill.

The type of fishing you do depends on the season (summer is best). The salmon season runs from mid-February through mid-November; rock cod and bass fish all year. Rock cod provides the biggest catches and will take you the farthest out on the Pacific—about 32 miles, to the Farallone Islands. Salmon fishing is done about 15 miles outside the Golden Gate, and bass fishing is done in the San Francisco Bay. Make your reservation at least a day in advance at either of these agencies:

Muni Bait Shop North Point and Polk Streets, across from Ghirardelli Square. Phone 673-9815.

Sport Fishing Center 300 Jefferson Street, next to the piers along Fisherman's Wharf. Phone 771-2800.

51 *See the History of the World as Viewed by a Grape*

Don't know anything about wine? A half hour in the Wine Museum of San Francisco and you'll be something of a semi-authority, able to hold fleeting conversation with even the snootiest of wine stewards.

The Wine Museum of San Franicsco first toured America for ten years as an exhibit celebrating "500 Years of Wine in the Arts" before it was settled on Fisherman's Wharf in 1974. Once there, it became the first permanent museum of its kind in the country, serving notice that America was at last ready to take itself seriously as a producer of fine wines. The museum collection is interesting and authoritative, enlivened by snatches of poetry, prose and sundry praise about the gift of the vine.

The Wine Museum of San Francisco is at 633 Beach Street. It's open Tue.-Sat. 11 a.m.-5 p.m., and Sunday noon-5 p.m. Guided tours are offered daily, 2-4 p.m. Phone 673-6990. Free.

52 *HEY, MISTER, THAT'S ME THERE IN THE JUKEBOX*

The warm summer sun draws them out like freckles: a trumpet-tooting gorilla, dancers, jugglers, mimes, all manner of musicians and magicians and . . . The Human Jukebox, picked in a 1973 *Wall Street Journal* poll as the most memorable monument in San Francisco.

106

Feed The Human Jukebox a quarter, press up your favorite song and stand back as Grimes Posnikov — aka The Human Jukebox — swings into action. Up comes the hatch, out pops a trumpet, down gets Posnikov on the tune of your selection, and back down goes the hatch. Darndest thing you ever saw.

Oh, yeah — don't bother trying to engage The Human Jukebox in idle chit-chat. Grimes Posnikov is also head of the Society for the Advancement of Non-Verbal Communication.

You'll usually find The Human Jukebox at Beach and Larkin Streets, across from the main entrance to Ghirardelli Square. He's there most summer days; and as the spirit moves him, during the winter.

CHINATOWN

CHINATOWN

Unlike Fisherman's Wharf, Chinatown is not a tourist send-up trading on a romanticized name (well, excepting for the ubiquitous Oriental Bazaars along Grant Avenue). Chinatown is a very real community, having some 80,000 residents jammed into an area eighteen square blocks small, a density ten times the city average. Chinatown is self-contained, governed largely from within, with its own language, customs and holidays. And problems as well, perhaps not readily apparent, but very real just the same.

Now this is certainly not meant to scare you away from Chinatown. Go, but with a heightened sense of the unique Chinese experience in San Francisco. It goes like this:

During the first twenty years after gold was discovered in California, some 100,000 Chinese passed through San Francisco on their way to the diggin's. After the gold gave out, Chinese laborers were still imported in wholesale numbers to make up most of the labor force that built the Transcontinental Railroad, planted the first California wineries, and cut the trees that built San Francisco.

By 1882, however, the work had given out and the Chinese who returned to San Francisco encountered a vicious backlash. Further immigration from China was sealed off. Those Chinese already here were forced to band together for their own protection in a homogeneous community along San Francisco's waterfront. This area for a time was called "Little Canton," after the Chinese seaport where most of the Chinese immigrants came from, but it later became known as Chinatown. Ironically, as the City filled out and around Chinatown, the once-worthless wharf property became some of the most valuable land in San Francisco. This caused a lot of low rumbling about re-locating Chinatown. There was even a concerted effort after the

Earthquake of 1906, but the Chinese built quickly to hold their ground. Unfortunately, they didn't have time to incorporate many elements of Chinese design into their new buildings. It wasn't until after they were safely in place that a few Oriental-style buildings went up. The most dramatic is the Bank of Canton at 743 Washington Street, just off Grant Avenue (it was originally built as a Chinese telephone exchange). Another eleventh-hour touch are the distinctive street lights along Grant Avenue. And something you might recognize if you rock n' roll is the intersection of Grant and Pacific. That's where the Doobie Brothers snapped the album cover photo for their *Takin' it to the Streets* album.

Here are a few tips to help you enjoy Chinatown:

Most of the tourist action in Chinatown is along the eight-block stretch of Grant Avenue between Bush and Broadway. However, the main street for the natives of Chinatown is Stockton Street, one block up from Grant. Check it out, too. Be sure to pop into some of the fish markets, grocery stores and alleys for the undiluted Chinatown. Try also to spend as much of one full day in Chinatown as possible, including at least one meal. If you want to take a guided tour of Chinatown—not a bad idea, actually—check out "Guided Tours" (#90). And don't forget to use your chopsticks!

Here's what to look for in Chinatown:

53 Look in on a Fortune Cookie Factory

A half a block up from Grant Avenue you'll find a dark, forboding passageway called Ross Alley. If you head into the block-long alley, you'll encounter a traditional preserve of ancient Chinatown wisdom: a fortune cookie factory.

Well, mature person that you are, you might as well know that you aren't going to find any venerable soothsayer inside. Rather, the forecast of a thousand futures is left to a couple of disinterested old ladies who stuff anonymous slips of paper into tiny cookie patties that come, cooked and cut, out of an assembly line cookie oven. "He who would expect to find ancient Chinese wiseman is very dumb cookie indeed."

The Golden Gate Fortune Cookie Company is at 56 Ross Alley, between Washington and Jackson Streets, half a block up from Grant Avenue. It's open seven days a week from 9 a.m.-8 p.m. You can also buy a bag of cookies on the premises.

54 I'M A WRITER, NOT A FIREFIGHTER

Back in the early days of Chinatown, residents followed an ancient Chinese custom by burning all their written documents after they had served their purpose. The sacred ashes were then taken out to sea to be dispersed in a small burst of ceremony.

Over time the residents of Chinatown forgot about this custom, as well as the *Non Wah Sher* (Society of Beautiful Writing), where the character assassinations were carried out. But a local historian, digging around Chinatown, rediscovered the small furnace building at the edge of Chinatown. It was thereafter deemed an appropriate place to house the Chinese Historical Society of America, the first of its kind in the country. In truth, the modest collection of Chinatown artifacts and photographs is only marginally interesting, but it makes a good reason to walk the length of Grant Avenue before you double back or head into North Beach.

The Chinese Historical Society of America is at the very northern edge of Chinatown at 17 Adler Place (the last street off Grant Avenue before it hits Broadway). It's open Wed.-Sun. 1-5 p.m. Phone 391-1188. Free.

55 VISIT A REAL-LIVE HERB SHOP

Having a hard time filling your prescription for monkey's blood or mice wine? You're in luck, because you can get just what the doctor ordered at any of the herb shops scattered throughout Chinatown.

Two of the most interesting are within half a block of each other on Washington Street, just off Grant Avenue. The Superior Trading Company at 839 Washington is well-lit, well-marked and antiseptic —clearly no way to run an herb shop. Tai Fung Wo and Company at 857 Washington (look for the deer skull in the window) is more what you'd expect an herb shop to be—dark, murky and musty. The drawers aren't marked—the herbist *knows* where everything is, and the sale is rung up on an abacus, a Chinese adding machine.

In the event that you're not quite sure just what ails you, go for the cure-all: ginseng root. Even at $80 an ounce, it's still a lot easier to swallow than monkey blood.

56 *Visit a Chinese Temple*

You can catch another glimpse of orthodox Chinese life at the Tin How and Kong Chow temples in Chinatown. Temples such as these —combining popular Taoist and Buddhist beliefs—were common throughout China until they were banned after the 1949 Communist Revolution. These two Chinatown temples are among the few remaining temples in the world. For a generation of older Chinese, they provide a fading link with their homeland.

The Kong Chow Temple was the first Chinese place of worship in the United States. It's housed now in a starched-white fourth floor room at 855 Stockton Street, corner of Clay Street. A much funkier temple is the Tin How Temple at 125 Waverly Place, in the heart of Chinatown. You'll pick up the scent of incense as you get close and should have no trouble following your nose to the temple's fourth-floor loft. (Chinese temples are always on the top floor of their building so that nothing can come between them and heaven.) "Tin How" translates to "Empress of Heaven." She's considered the protector of travelers, just in case you've got a long trip ahead of you.

Both temples are open seven days a week, 10 a.m.-4 p.m. There are attendants at each who will explain the intricate temple ceremony. Both temples are free, but encourage and accept contributions.

57 Dine *Dim Sum*

If you're about ready to dropkick your chopsticks, try eating your next Chinese meal with your fingers. You're perfectly welcome to in one of the various Chinatown tea houses that serve dim sum lunches.

The lunchtime tradition of dim sum—it translates to "Little Jewel"—originated in Canton, China. Legend has it that a Chinese empress was so taken with small foods and pastries—hors d'oeuvres, if you will—that she commanded her chef to invent all manner of the little delicacies. Over the years the array of treats has been somewhat standardized. They are served now from a cart that is wheeled around to your table. You pick and choose from the tray, and pay according to the number of plates on your table at the end of the meal. Dim sum is a delightful way to take lunch and a good way to sample Chinese food without being stuck with too much of a mistake.

Following is a list of the tea houses in Chinatown that serve dim sum lunches:

The Golden Pavilion 800 Sacramento Street 392-2334
Hang Ah Tea Room 1 Hang Ah Street (off Sacramento near Stockton Street) 982-5686
Golden Dragon Restaurant 816-822 Washington Street 398-3920
Louie's of Grant Avenue 1014 Grant Avenue 982-5762
Canton Tea House 1108 Stockton Street 982-1032

Asia Garden Restaurant   772 Pacific Avenue   398-5112
Tung Fong Restaurant   808 Pacific Avenue   362-7115
Hong Kong Tea House   835 Pacific Avenue   391-6365
Yank Sing Restaurant   671 Broadway   781-1111

58 SEE THE WORLD'S RUDEST WAITER

He baits and berates male customers and shamelessly hustles every woman who enters his domain. He'll throw you a load of chopsticks with a brusque "Dry!" or spirit away your date to help him wait on tables. He's a refreshingly irreverent wit and an absolutely crazed madman. His name is Edsel Ford Fung (really), and he's held forth from the second floor of Sam Wo's in Chinatown since the 1940s, even inspiring such bad poetry as:

> *He stomps his feet, he screams he shouts*
> *But in the end it will all work out.*
> *Behind that pair of squinty eyes*
> *You'll find a man who is very wise.*
> *People he knows both inside and out*
> *He will misjudge no one and there is no doubt.*
>
> *—Author Unknown*

And so on. Except for Edsel Ford Fung, Sam Wo's is a standard Chinese jook house (jook is a thick rice soup), frequented mostly by locals. Now you know about it. Enter at your own risk, however, and be forewarned to "Be precise!"

Sam Wo's is at 813 Washington Street (just off Grant Avenue). Edsel Ford Fung works the second floor dining room. Open Mon.-Sat. 11 a.m.-3 a.m. Phone 982-0596.

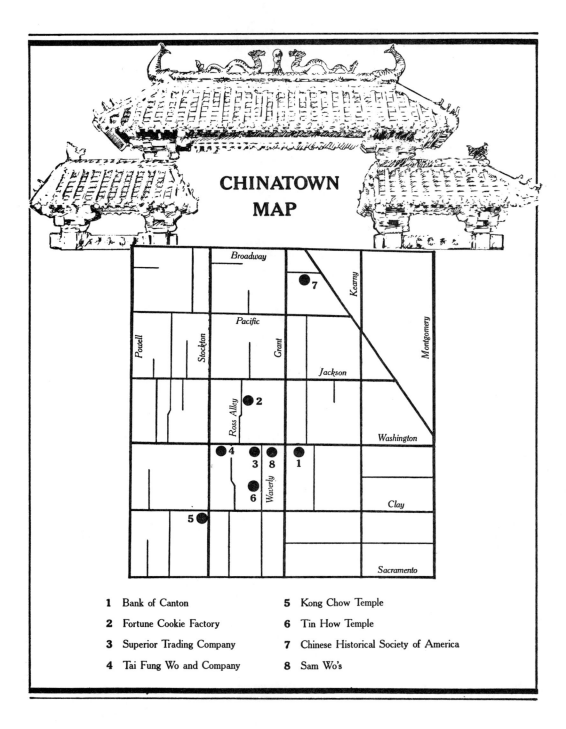

CHINATOWN MAP

1 Bank of Canton		**5** Kong Chow Temple
2 Fortune Cookie Factory		**6** Tin How Temple
3 Superior Trading Company		**7** Chinese Historical Society of America
4 Tai Fung Wo and Company		**8** Sam Wo's

NORTH BEACH

North Beach

First of all, there is no "North Beach" per se. The small sandy beach on the tip of town that North Beach pinched its name from is gone and long-forgotten. Over the years, such generic successors as "Little Italy" and "The Latin Quarter" have been alternately used to refer to the area bounded by Chinatown and Fisherman's Wharf. Neither has taken, however, because North Beach is more accurately a state of mind, a colorful pastiche of three separate neighborhoods, each with its own pace and pulse.

There is, of course, Broadway, the neon netherworld between Chinatown and North Beach. Broadway is the spiritual successor to the Barbary Coast, although it was never a part of it. For most of its existence, in fact, Broadway even had pretensions to propriety. Carol Doda blew that cover in 1964, transforming the once-timid Italian street into a veritable bay of nipples. The heart of the action now is the head-on collision of Broadway and Columbus (see #13).

Just around the corner from Broadway and Columbus is Upper Grant Avenue, the fossilized remains of the heady Beat Generation. The soul and conscience of the Beats is and was Lawrence Ferlinghetti's City Lights Bookstore at 261 Columbus, near Broadway (see #12). Most of the action was strung out along a three block stretch of Upper Grant Avenue, between Columbus and Union Streets. San Francisco's Beat Era is described in lavish detail under number 30.

Finally, there's Italian North Beach, which encompasses the other two geographically and imbues the whole area with its continental style and blue collar substance. The heart of Italian North Beach is Washington Square, a pleasant park on Columbus between Union and Filbert Streets; its main artery is Columbus, which starts at the Transamerica Pyramid and ends in Fisherman's Wharf, roughly the boundaries of North Beach itself.

North Beach is the essence of San Francisco. You'll be charmed right down to your toes. Here's a starter list of things to do in North Beach. Don't let it limit you, though. You'll find as much to do in North Beach as you have time to do it.

59 *Look Into North Beach's Past*

The history of North Beach has been neatly catalogued in the North Beach Museum, in the heart of North Beach. The photos, exhibits and artifacts change, but the people and places pictured remain the same: solid, substantial and here-to-stay. The small museum is a quick and convenient way to peek into North Beach's past before you head into its present.

The North Beach Museum is on the mezzanine floor of the Eureka Federal Savings Building, 1435 Stockton Street, near Columbus Avenue. It's open Mon.-Thur. 9 a.m.-4:30 p.m., Friday 9 a.m.-6 p.m., and Saturday 9 a.m.-1 p.m. Phone 391-6218. Free.

60 SNIFF OUT THE REAL FLAVOR OF NORTH BEACH

The best tour guide in North Beach is your nose. Follow it and you'll be led into the true preserves of Italian heritage: the kitchens of North Beach. Here's a starter's list of seven. (For a little eye excitement, poke your nose into the Caffe Sport, 574 Green Street, or the Golden Spike, 527 Columbus Avenue.)

1. The **Caferata Ravioli Factory** at 700 Columbus Avenue transforms plain, ordinary pasta into tender little clouds of ravioli. You're welcome to look in on the miraculous transformation through Caferata's giant picture windows, Mon.-Fri. 10 a.m.-3 p.m.

2. Across the street at 733 Columbus is the **Graffeo Coffee House**, but if you have to be told you have a cold. That's because the rich aroma of coffee begins to greet you about two doors away. The Graffo has been roasting coffee since 1935, longer than anyone else in North Beach. You can catch them at it throughout the day, Monday through Saturday.

3. Now double back along Washington Square on Union Street, to **Malvina's Coffee Shop** at 512 Union Street (corner of Grant Avenue). The upstairs is a pleasant, unassuming coffee shop. Downstairs is where Malvina's takes care of business, grinding and roasting its own coffee. They roast at various times throughout the day, seven days a week. If you call a day ahead of time, however, they'll be glad to reserve a command roast for you. Phone 392-4736.

4. Two blocks further up Grant Avenue, at the corner of Vallejo Street, you'll find the consummate cup of cappuccino. **Caffe Trieste** is run with a passion by the Giotta family. During the mornings, the Giottas roast their coffee on a huge antique roaster that they tracked down in Germany and shipped back to San Francisco for the pure love of it. During the rest of the day, they share the fruits of their labor in the attached coffee shop, a longtime haunt of the North Beach literati. But Saturday afternoons at one o'clock is the best time of all to stop by Caffe Trieste. That's when the entire Giotta family gathers in the coffee shop to perform opera for their friends and customers. Caffe Trieste is open seven days a week until at least 8 p.m. Phone 982-2605.

5. Next, point your nose in the direction of **Molinari's**, an Italian delicatessen at 373 Columbus. Molinari's window is filled with a fabulous array of Italian herbs, wines, waters, noodles, breads and olive oil tins (which make great containers once drained of their original responsibility). All this before you even set foot inside the place. Set your senses for "Assault." Molinari's Delicatessen is open Mon.-Sat., 8 a.m.-6 p.m. Phone 421-2337.

6. **R. Iacopi and Company**, 1460 Grant Avenue, is the oldest butcher shop in San Francisco. On most Thursdays and Fridays, you can drop in to watch as the butchers make their sausage—by hand. The process involves squeezing ground hamburger and sundry pork parts into pork intestines. If you've got the stomach for it, phone ahead to 421-0757.

7. Then there's the greatest San Francisco tradition of them all, which is on daily display at the **Boudin Bakery**, 160 Jefferson Street, in the heart of Fisherman's Wharf. Behind the giant picture windows, the small miracle of sourdough takes place each day. The bakers themselves won't tell you too much about the process (see #22), but you can divine what you will from 8 a.m. to 2 p.m., any day of the week. The best time is around 8:30 a.m. when the dough is mixed. Phone 928-1849.

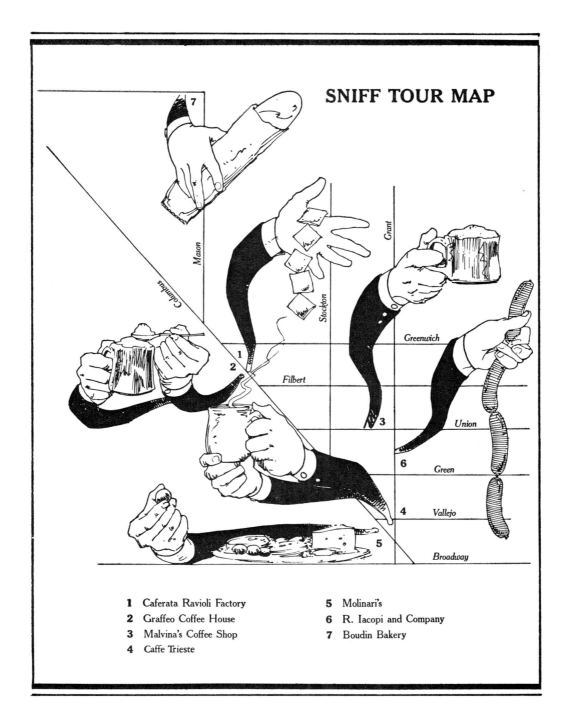

SNIFF TOUR MAP

1 Caferata Ravioli Factory

2 Graffeo Coffee House

3 Malvina's Coffee Shop

4 Caffe Trieste

5 Molinari's

6 R. Iacopi and Company

7 Boudin Bakery

61 Watch the Stars Come In at Wim's

The Brown Derby it ain't. In fact, a plain, undistinguished counter-top restaurant is all that it is. So what makes Wim's the best place in San Francisco to star-gaze?

The walls give you a clue. They're loaded with pictures from *Apocalypse Now*, *THX 1138*, the two *Godfathers* and sundry Academy Awards nights. There's even a rare photo of Marlon Brando sitting for his interview for *The Godfather*. Yup, what separates Wim's is its owner, Francis Coppola. Coppola's offices are near the restaurant, which is why the producer conducts a lot of his business over lunch in the booth in the back. In fact, The Booth—the only one in the place —is given out only on Coppola's orders. If anyone's back there, you can bet he's Someone.

Wim's is on the cusp of North Beach and the Financial District in a triangular building formed by the intersection of Columbus Avenue and Kearny Street. It's open Mon.-Fri. 7 a.m.-3 p.m. Phone 421-3481.

UNION STREET

UNION STREET

Union Street is the quintessential street of San Francisco. The six block stretch of Union between Gough and Steiner Streets has undergone a cinderella transformation from a sleepy neighborhood into a world fashion place. By day, shoppers stroll chic to chic. By night, the sleek bars and restaurants provide singles with a place to meet and mingle.

It hasn't always been so. In fact, there is little in Union Street's past to suggest that it might ever become more than an accessory to good taste. A small lake that (if it were still around) would lap up against the sidewalk of the present Union Street became known as "Washerwoman's Lagoon," after the housewives and washerwomen who used to ring the lake on laundry day. The first large scale migration into the area was by cows, who grazed the green valley and supplied milk for nearby San Francisco. Eventually there were some thirty dairies in Cow Hollow, as the area became known, and a burgeoning slaughterhouse industry. It didn't take long before the affluent residents up the hill looked down their offended noses and banished the cows, filled in Washerwoman's Lagoon and covered Cow Hollow over in Victorians.

Which is how things stood up until the 1950s, when Union Street went into belated bloom. Several antique shops quietly took up residence alongside the homes and neighborhood shops on Union Street. This inconspicuous first wave was quickly followed by a very conspicuous assault of boutiques, bars, restaurants and people. Like a snake shedding its skin, moldy houses suddenly came to life in a burst of color. By the mid-'60s, Union Street had lost all semblance of residential decorum. Fortunately, its honor didn't suffer too much. Most of the businesses on the street have been honed out of a Victorian or custom-built to fit on the street, with a few glaring exceptions (most notably the Wells Fargo Bank at 1900 Union and a shopping complex at 2001 Union Street).

Union Street is pure fiction, but it's fun. Few places feel more decadently "San Francisco"—it's the irresistible combination of Victorian charm and high-fashion. Plan an afternoon accentuated by a meal, but be forewarned: most of the shops and restaurants on Union Street range from expensive on up. Also, parking is the pits. However, Union Street is just an invigorating walk from Fisherman's Wharf, or either a short cab ride or quick bus trip from downtown.

62 WHAT GOD HAS JOINED TOGETHER LET NO MAN PUT ASUNDER

The most charming and colorful building on all of Union Street is at 1980 Union, between Laguna and Buchanan Streets. If you look closely, you'll notice that what looks like a single structure is actually two identical houses, separated only by a common wall. They're called the "Wedding Houses." Legend has it that they were commissioned by an extra-frugal father for his two newlywed daughters. Legend is silent on what the two grooms thought of the arrangement. The houses have since been hollowed out and filled with the variety of shops and restaurants that you see.

63 See San Francisco's Most Unusual House

If you stop at the corner of Union and Webster Streets and look down a block to 2963 Webster, you'll see San Francisco's most bizarre house. The maroon and gray structure belongs to the Vendanta

Society. Vendanta is the highest of the six Hindu systems of religion, which accounts for the rather unusual roof on the house. You may not be able to see all of it, but the roof has a European style castle tower, a bulbed dome in the style of Bengal temples, an octagonal dome in honor of the Shiva temples, a cluster of pointed domes that represents a temple of Banras, and a larger dome in the style of the Taj Mahal. The house is closed to the public.

Listen, in times like these, it is a wise man indeed who covers as many bets as possible.

DOWNTOWN

DOWNTOWN

In 1976, the American Revolution Bicentennial Administration cited San Francisco as "simply the best example of urban renewal in the country." The reason for downtown San Francisco's vigorous constitution is simply that it has never lost a drop of the lifeblood of great cities: people. From their pioneer past to the present, San Franciscans have conducted their most significant business and reserved their most important shopping for downtown. The majority of San Francisco's clubs and theatres are located in or near the downtown area, as are a great many of the City's finest restaurants. And downtown is also where you'll find a bounty of San Francisco's unannounced surprises, as evidenced by the list below:

64 See Where Tony Bennett Left His Heart

When you think of San Francisco, you naturally think of Fisherman's Wharf, the Golden Gate Bridge . . . and Tony Bennett warbling "To be where little cable cars/Climb halfway to the stars." "I Left My Heart in San Francisco" was good for Tony (who actually lives in Southern California) and good for San Francisco, which proclaimed it the official city song in 1969. The City then gathered up a few mementos of the famous song and put them on display in the San Francisco Visitors Information Center. There you'll see Tony's gold record, the original manuscript, and a note pad that was used to scratch out a rough draft of the song.

Now take a good look at that note pad. You'll be mildly amazed to learn that the song's signature line almost came out as "I long to see the cable cars/Climb past the sidewalk stalls of flowers."

The San Francisco Visitor Information Center is next to the Powell Street BART entrance. From the Powell Street cable car turn-around, take the escalator down to a small plaza. You'll see the Visitor Information Center straight ahead of you. It's open Mon.-Fri. 9 a.m.-5 p.m., Saturday 9 a.m.-3 p.m., and Sunday 10 a.m.- 2 p.m. Phone 626-5500. Free.

65 STROLL MAIDEN LANE

And laugh knowingly at the irony of it all. During the heyday of the Barbary Coast, Maiden Lane—or Morton Street, as it was known then—was lined solid with whorehouses. As the street gradually overcame its randy past and boutiques moved in to take the place of bordellos, "Morton" was changed to "Maiden" in hopes of sparking a new era of chasteness.

Both blocks of the abbreviated street are a delightful and human break from the big city bustle around it. Of special interest is the Helga Howie boutique at 140 Maiden Lane. The small building was designed in 1948 by Frank Lloyd Wright, who left his personal monogram in a red brick to the left of the store entrance. The striking building is considered to be one of his small masterpieces, foreshadowing the work he did on the Guggenheim Museum in New York City.

Maiden Lane runs off Union Square where an alley would be. It starts at Stockton Street, on the east side of Union Square, and ends two blocks later at Kearny Street.

66 SEE THE WORLD'S ONLY TATTOO MUSEUM

Summon up your curiosity and call on your courage for a visit to the "wrong" side of Market Street to see another San Francisco original: the world's first and only tattoo museum. The unique gallery is a labor of love for curator Lyle Tuttle, who is himself tattooed from neck to ankle (several candid photos of the multicolored Tuttle are on display).

Most of the rest of the small museum is taken up with a variety of intricate designs from the Orient, and examples of the primitive equipment used before electricity and sterilization made it a "civilized" art. There's also a rack of the ubiquitous "war and women" designs that today stare in muted glory from under T-shirts and atop beer bellies all over the U.S. (it's estimated that 65 percent of all American sailors during World War II acquired a tattoo).

However, what's most intriguing is what you can't see: several human hides, preserved for their intricate designs, that Lyle Tuttle has locked away. Sorry—you'll have to wrangle a viewing for yourself.

The Tattoo Art Museum adjoins Lyle Tuttle's downtown studio at 30 Seventh Street (next to the Greyhound Bus Depot). It's open Mon.-Sat. noon-4 p.m. Phone 864-9798. Admission.

67 SEE A SPOT THAT ALMOST MADE HISTORY (AND ANOTHER THAT DID)

On 23 September 1975, President Gerald Ford stepped out of the St. Francis Hotel on Union Square by a side entrance on Post Street.

Standing in the crowd directly across Post Street in front of a United Airlines ticket office was Sara Jane Moore. As Ford reached his limousine, Moore raised her arm and took dead aim on the President of the United States. Standing next to Moore in the crowd was ex-Marine Oliver Sipple. Seeing what was about to happen, Sipple lunged for Moore's arm just as she squeezed off a shot, knocking the assassination bullet off its course and probably saving the life of the President. Ford was hustled into his car and out of California after the second attempt on his life in as many weeks.

Another president wasn't so lucky. As his wife read aloud to him on the night of 2 August 1923, President Warren G. Harding died in the Presidential Suite of the Palace Hotel in San Francisco. Harding had taken ill several days earlier, but was thought to be improving at the time of his death. Because of that, a nasty rumor has lately surfaced, which attributes President Harding's death to Mrs. Harding, in a baby-with-the-bathwater attempt to spare her husband the political embarrassment of the unfolding Teapot Dome scandal. History will never know.

The stately Palace Hotel at Fifth and Market Streets, downtown, has since become the Sheraton Palace. The Presidential Suite, Room 860, is still kept up for visiting presidents and lesser mortals for a mere $250 a night. If you need a place to stay tonight, give them a call at 392-8600.

68 TAKE THE BEST FREE RIDE IN TOWN

Pressed for time, money or cheap thrills? Then try the quickest and most enlightening tour of San Francisco. It's the PDF Tour (Press Desired Floor), aka the outside elevators of the St. Francis Hotel. Hop one, preferably alone or with your own party, and you'll shoot thirty-two floors straight up over Union Square. Actually, the ride is so smooth that the City just seems to stretch out before you, offering an unparalled view of Coit Tower, Mt. Tamalpais and the Bay Bridge. During the day, you can even dawdle at the top. By night, the thirty-second floor turns into a plush disco, and you might be hustled on your way.

You can't miss the St. Francis Hotel—it sits right on Union Square. The outside elevators are at the far end of the main lobby. Ask at the desk if you have any trouble locating them.

69 Discover San Francisco's Most Famous Address

Thirty floors above Union Square in an otherwise basic rooftop bar you come upon a startling discovery: the legendary 221B Baker Street, address of Sherlock Holmes. You deduce this from the various Holmesian effects scattered about the room: a Persian slipper, a non-Canonical calabash pipe, portraits of General Gordon and Henry Ward Beecher adorning the wall. A table set with the evening fare —wine and meat pie—testify to your hosts having only recently been called out, no doubt to foil the insidious Professor Moriarity. You sit down anyway to enjoy the hospitality of your legendary hosts, breaking out a bottle of Holmes' favorite scotch (Glen Aiddich) and Watson's preferred cognac (Napoleon Grade Fine Champagne) to assuage the tedium of the wait. From the looks of things, they could be gone a very long while.

You'll discover the delightful—albeit unlikely—recreation of Sherlock Holmes' London home in the Sherlock Holmes Bar on the thirtieth floor of the Holiday Inn Union Square, at the corner of Sutter and Powell Streets, downtown. It's open seven days a week, 11 a.m.-1:30 a.m. Phone 398-8900.

70 RAISE A TOAST TO THE GHOST OF BLACK BART

Who says crime doesn't pay? The Black Bart Saloon in the Hotel San Franciscan is named after a charming rogue out of San Francisco's past who has come to symbolize the lawless spirit of the times. For eight years during the late 1870s and early 1880s, Black Bart waged a personal war on the Wells Fargo stagecoach line, holding up twenty-seven stages as easily as he held up his pants. Bart's calling card was always a short poem, signed by "Black Bart the PO8" (po-et, get it?). One of his better ones goes:

I rob the rich to feed the poor
Which hardly is a sin
A widow ne'er knocked at my door
But what I let her in.
So blame me not for what I've done
I don't deserve your curses
And if for any cause I'm hung
Let it be for my verses.

On his twenty-eighth job, Black Bart slipped up and left an incriminating handkerchief behind. Wells Fargo agents were able to trace the laundry mark back to one Charles E. Bolton, a not-so-surprisingly wealthy San Franciscan who had explained away his frequent out-of-town trips to mining business.

Bolton fessed up, did four years in San Quentin and then disappeared forever. But the spirit of the gentleman outlaw and a few examples of his poetry are kept alive at the Black Bart Saloon in the Hotel San Franciscan, Eighth and Market Streets, downtown. Phone 626-8000.

FINANCIAL DISTRICT

Financial District

Montgomery Street, the heart of San Francisco's Financial District, is called "The Wall Street of the West." It comes by the name quite honestly. From the first flush of the Gold Rush to the very present, the banks of Montgomery Street have stored a good deal of the wealth of the West. The largest bank in the world, Bank of America, was founded in San Francisco. Today, its headquarters rise fifty-two stories above Montgomery Street on California Street. (If the striking skyscraper looks a little familiar, it's because it was the "Towering Inferno" in the movie of the same name.) Elsewhere in the Financial District are the 12th District Federal Reserve Bank and the Pacific Coast Stock Exchange.

If the Financial District sounds like its almost all business, it almost all is. But close at hand are some of San Francisco's oldest and best restaurants and a couple of points of genuine interest, to wit:

71 Elevate to the Top of the Pyramid

If your curiosity has been pricked by the giant pyramid that stands square in the middle of San Francisco's skyline, you might want to wander over for a visit. The Transamerica Pyramid is world headquarters for the Transamerica Corporation ("We're the people in the pyramid"), which includes United Artists, Occidental Life Insurance and Budget Rent-A-Car.

The Transamerica Pyramid is forty-eight floors or 853 feet tall, including the crowning 212-foot spire (which is kept lit at night). The

floor space shrinks from 22,000 square feet on the fifth floor to a mere 2,000 square feet by the forty-eighth. The windowless protrusions on either side of the pyramid house an elevator shaft and a smoke tower. The only floor above the lobby open to the public is the twenty-seventh floor observation deck. Unfortunately, the view isn't any great shakes, and the whole interior of the pyramid is somewhat underwhelming.

Infinitely more interesting is the pyramid's predecessor on the spot, a squat, four-story building called the Montgomery Block. From 1951 through 1959, the "Monkey" Block was the hub of San Francisco's hub bub. It was the first fireproof building built in the City, and, as such, carried on most of San Francisco's important business. After business moved out, a second wave moved in, featuring some of the most important names in American letters. Mark Twain, Bret Harte, Robert Louis Stevenson, Rudyard Kipling, Jack London, Ambroce Bierce and William Randolph Hearst all either had office space in the building or regularly sallied on down to drink and dally at The Bank Exchange, the Montgomery Block's legendary bar. The Bank Exchange's substantial reputation rested on a couple of heavenly nectars known as "Pisco Punch" and "Button Punch." The recipe for both drinks died with their creator, but Rudyard Kipling offered this fair approximation of Button Punch: "It is compounded of cherub's wings, the glory of a tropical dawn, the red clouds of sunset, and the fragments of lost epics by dead masters."

A young doctor named Sun Yat-sen plotted the successful overthrow of the Manchu Dynasty and later wrote the Chinese Constitution from a second floor office in the Montgomery Block. Newspaper publisher James King of William staggered to the Monkey Block to die after being shot by political enemy James Casey, prompting the most famous hanging of the Vigilance Committee. In the basement of the building was a Turkish Bath frequented by Mark Twain during his years in San Francisco. The proprietor of the bath was named Tom Sawyer.

The Transamerica Pyramid is on Montgomery Street, between Clay and Washington Streets. The twenty-seventh floor observation deck is open Mon.-Fri. 8:30 a.m.-4 p.m. Free.

72 SEE THE ROOT OF ALL THAT EVIL

Money. If you like it, you can't help but be moved by the collection of gold and coins compiled by and on display at the Bank of California. There's a lot of reverential discussion of the great California and Nevada gold and silver mines, as well as displays on most every aspect of money (except how to get it). But the genuine showstopper here is the privately minted coins. Not only do they predate inflation (before people started taking the government's word for it, a coin had to be worth its weight in gold), but the privately minted coins were also infinitely more creative than the standardized government issues.

The Bank of California Gold and Coin Museum is downstairs in the Bank of California, 400 California Street (corner of Sansome Street). It's open banking days and hours: Mon.-Fri. 10 a.m.-3 p.m. Phone 765-0400. Free.

73 See the World's First Modern Building

The future of twentieth century architecture was forecast way back in 1918 in San Francisco's Financial District. It was there that the world's first glass skyscraper was built . . . sort of. Technology not being quite up to architect Willis Polk's vision, the Hallidie Building turns out to be a delicate glass "curtain" hung out in front of a regular steel frame building. But it still shocked the architectural community down to their support socks, causing them to ignore San Francisco's innovative lead for more than three decades. It wasn't until 1950 that the glass skyscraper came of age with the construction of the U.N.

Secretariat Building in New York City. Since then, the idea has sort of caught on. The Hallidie Building is now properly revered as a milestone in American architecture.

The Hallidie Building still looks refreshingly light on its feet. You can see it at 130 Sutter Street, between Montgomery and Kearny Streets. Look for a post office on the first floor.

74 Go to the Moon

So what else were you planning to do today?

Walk to 595 Market at the corner of Second and Market Streets. There you'll see a Rand McNally map store with a huge geophysical globe in the front window. This globe is purported to be the most accurate relief globe ever made. It is certainly one of the biggest. How big is it? Well, you'd have to cross Second Street just to approximate a trip to the moon. But the view back to the globe-earth is unimpeded by clouds, an advantage Neil Armstrong never had (even if he didn't have to wait for the light to change before he could make his return voyage).

By the way, if you'd like to buy the globe, it goes for a mere $25,975 —FOB New York, but of course.

GOLDEN GATE PARK

GOLDEN GATE PARK

In 1873, after San Francisco had set aside one thousand acres of dunes for a showcase park, a newspaper editorial took the City to task for even imagining that a park could be sculpted out of "a dreary waste of shifting sandhills where a blade of grass cannot be raised without four posts to keep it from blowing away. . . ." Well, San Francisco has enjoyed the last laugh for over a century now, because Golden Gate Park is every bit the showcase park it was intended to be. Moreover, it even set off something of a revolution in park design. Back in the nineteenth century, proper parks were flat. The rolling dunes that became Golden Gate Park were decidedly not. Park architects convinced the City to let nature have its way, hedging their bet slightly by suggesting the ease with which an enemy attacker or cold ocean breeze could roll unchecked across a flat park. San Francisco quickly agreed.

After only twenty years, Golden Gate Park was shaping up so nicely that San Francisco decided to show it off. The California Midwinter Fair (San Francisco also wanted to brag about its weather) of 1894/95 left the seeds for today's "Heart of the Park," the impressive cluster of museums and gardens strung around the Music Concourse (just look for the crewcut trees in front of a bandshell). On Sundays, this part of Golden Gate Park is closed to traffic, making it the natural place to start your visit. Remember, though, it's only a very small part of the park. If you want to see more, you'd do well to rent yourself some roller skates or a bicycle and just dig in. Don't worry about getting lost—although the park is three miles long, it's only half a mile wide, so you're never more than a quarter of a mile from civilization by heading either due north or south.

Following is a starter list of things to do in Golden Gate Park. Left to your own devices, however, you'd still come up with a day's worth of activities, easy. (The M.H. deYoung Museum and the California Academy of Sciences are described under "Culture" on page 93.)

75 *Meditate in the Oriental Tea Garden*

The Oriental Tea Garden is the only exhibit that was retained after the Midwinter Fair of 1894/95. It was designed by an Australian, but was fittingly loved into full bloom by three generations of a Japanese family. If you beat the foot traffic that picks up during the day, you'll have your senses scrubbed clean by the quiet walk that leads you ultimately to the foot of Buddha.

The Oriental Tea Garden is open seven days a week, 8 a.m.-6 p.m. Free.

76 RECITE SHAKESPEARE IN THE PARK

Tucked away near the Academy of Natural Sciences is a fascinating little garden. All of the trees and plants in the Garden of Shakespeare's Flowers share the distinction of being mentioned by Shakespeare in his prose and poetry. If you can't quite identify the plants from memory, the relevant quotations are etched onto a brick wall in the back of the garden. A map in the front of the garden pinpoints the plants by location. Also on the back wall is a green box, usually locked, which contains a bust of the bard cast from an actual death mask. There were only two copies ever made—the one in the park and another that stayed behind at Stratford-Upon-Avon. If you'd like to see the bust, call ahead at 558-4407 and ask for the Assistant Superintendent of Parks.

77 Take a Circular Stroll Through the Arboretum

The Arboretum is an unsung jewel in a city of well-sung splendors. The Arboretum (it means a place where plants are cultivated for scientific purposes, but don't let that put you off) is sixty carefully coiffured acres of plants and trees. All you have to do is grab one of the circular paths and follow your nose until you get dizzy or drunk on the beauty. (P.S.: If you're a jogger, you won't find a more pleasant run in all the City.)

The Arboretum is open Mon.-Fri. 8 a.m.-4:30 p.m., Saturday, Sundays and holidays 10 a.m.-5 p.m. Guided tours are offered daily at 1:30 p.m. Free.

78 RENT A GOOD TIME

Peddle, paddle or slip into a saddle for a rented trip through Golden Gate Park. Here's how and where:

ROLLER SKATE RENTALS

The best way to see the park, especially on a Sunday when there's no traffic. These days, the park is literally ringed with roller rental trucks. Rates at the various trucks and shops vary, but run around $1 per hour and $5 per day. Get there early, because if your size goes out you have to wait until it comes back in. Bring an ID.

Buffalo Skaters

These are the people who started it all. They operate out of a truck on the north side of the park at 8th and Fulton. You'll find them there for sure on weekends and holidays from 9 a.m.-5 p.m., and as the spirit moves them during the week in the summer. Phone 441-5698.

Skates on Haight

1818 Haight Street (one-half block from the park on the east side). Open seven days a week, 10 a.m.-6 p.m. Phone 752-8375.

Aji Cyclery

1251 9th Avenue (on the south side of the park near the Hall of Flowers). Open seven days a week, 9 a.m.-6 p.m. Phone 665-1394.

BICYCLE RENTALS

There are four bicycle rental shops ringing Golden Gate Park. Prices vary from shop to shop, but a three-speed will run you about $1.50 per hour; a five-speed, $1.75 per hour; and a ten-speed, $2.50 per hour. A tandem bike goes for about the same as a ten-speed. All require an ID and, occasionally, a small deposit.

Aji Cyclery

1251 9th Avenue (on the south side of the park near the Hall of Flowers). Open seven days a week, 9 a.m.-6 p.m. Phone 665-1394. Has three-, five- and ten-speeds, and tandems.

Avenue Cyclery

750 Stanyan Street (on the east side). Open Tues.-Sun. 9:30 a.m.-5:30 p.m. Phone 387-3155. Has three-, five- and ten-speeds.

The Bike Shop

4621 Lincoln Way (on the south side near the ocean). Open Mon., Wed., Fri.-Sun. 9:30 a.m.-5 p.m., Tues. and Thur. noon-5 p.m. Phone 665-3092. It has three-speeds only.

Lincoln Cyclery

> 772 Stanyan Street (on the east side). Open Wed.-Sat. 9 a.m.-5 p.m., Sunday 10:30 a.m.-5 p.m., Monday 9 a.m.-5 p.m. Phone 221-2415. They have three- and ten-speeds.

HORSE RENTALS

Just west of the Buffalo Paddock off Kennedy Drive is the Golden Gate Equestrian Center, where you can rent a horse. Fortunately, since you'd probably get lost anyway, you have to go out with a guide. The rate is $6 per hour. The stables are open seven days a week 9 a.m.-3 p.m., but get there early to avoid a wait (and call ahead on Monday just to be sure). Phone 664-9877. You also have to be over ten years old.

BOAT RENTALS

You can circle serene Stow Lake (near the "Heart of the Park") on your choice of an electric motor, pedal or row boat. The price for one or two people is $5.50 per hour for the electric motor boats, $4.50 per hour for the pedal boats and $4 per hour for the row boats (add 50¢ each hour for each additional mate). They're open Tues.-Sun. 9 a.m.-4 p.m. Phone 752-0347. The boat house is on the north end of Stow Lake.

THE BAY AND THE PACIFIC

79 GO AHEAD. BARE IT ALL AT A NUDE BEACH

So why not? A nude beach really isn't all that sexy. Ask any swimsuit manufacturer—they'll tell you that a one-piece or clinging bikini is far more provocative than the all-over body alone. Besides, you just plain can't beat the feeling of freedom when the sun, waves and wind simultaneously beat and blow over parts of your body that seem to be forever locked away inside your underwear. Go ahead—you have nothing to lose but your inhibitions.

Here in Northern California, a nude beach is theoretically any cove that you're willing to colonize. In practice, however, the official attitude—if not policies—of the various governing agencies is that nude bathers have their beaches and the general public has its own; if everyone keeps to his or her place, there's no problem. If a nude bather does happen to stray, he or she will most likely be told to dress and move on. Although the U.S. Park Rangers, administrators over most of the nude beaches in these parts, can hand out citations for "disorderly display," the actual number they give out annually amounts to "less than a handful."

There are three nude beaches within easy reach of San Francisco, as well as another one within the city limits. One beach is on private property, and the others are on either State or National Park Service land. If you want the two best and busiest, skip the rest and head either south to Edun Cove or north to Red Rocks Beach. If not, here's a description of each beach with directions:

IN SAN FRANCISCO

Land's End Beach
The only nude beach within the city limits. It's an ocean beach, just outside the Golden Gate Bridge, affording the bather a nice view of the bridge and the ships passing in and out of the harbor. Unfortunately, Land's End doesn't even come close to having anything you

might consider long stretches of white sand. It's close to home, however, and does have quite a bit of beach—such as it is. The beach is largely gay, but it's also used by couples and even a few brave families.

To Get There: Head west on Geary Avenue (towards the ocean) until you come to El Camino del Mar, the last intersection before the Cliff House (and one block past 47th—Seal Rocks Inn will be on your left). Take a right and head into the large parking lot. Walk down to the dirt path just below the parking lot and head to your right (towards the Golden Gate Bridge) for a good ways until you cross a small wooden bridge. There are several small paths that lead directly down to the beach at this point. The main beach is marked by several small rock windbreaks.

SOUTH OF SAN FRANCISCO

Edun Cove Beach

This is the most beautiful of all the nude beaches in the San Francisco area. It's also located on hassleless private land. The owner runs a parking concession above the beach and has even been thoughtful enough to provide outhouses and a stairway down to the beach. The beach itself is spectacular—a long, luxurious stretch of white sand nestled in a cove that's been carved out of the high hills around it. On a warm day, the beach is crowded with thousands of sun worshippers of all types—straight, gay, young, old, single or in twos.

To Get There: Take Highway 101 south out of San Francisco to the 280/Daly City turnoff. Take that until you get to the Pacifica/Highway 1 exit; proceed down Highway 1 through Pacifica, past Rockaway Beach, and several miles past the point where Highway 1 turns into a two-lane road. The beach is exactly three miles from the stoplight in Linda Mar (you'll see an A&W on your right at this point). You'll know you're at Edun Cove when you see an American flag and a sign that reads "Beach Parking." An adjacent nude beach is just up around the next bend—you'll be able to see that beach from the road (but then, so can everyone else). The drive to Edun Cove from San Francisco takes about thirty minutes. There's an admission charge for the parking lot.

NORTH OF SAN FRANCISCO

Rodeo Beach

A nice beach if you want to do some quiet, undisturbed nude bathing.
The largest part of the beach just below the Rodeo Lagoon is used by
the general public, but if you head south along the beach you'll find
some fairly secluded ocean front. The only drawback to the beach is
that it's frequently windy and tends to get cold very early.

*To Get There: Head north across the Golden Gate Bridge and imme-
diately take the Alexander Avenue exit. The first intersection you come
to will be Danes Drive (a more noticeable sign welcomes you to Forts
Barry, Baker and Cronkhite), which quickly becomes Bunker Road.
Take a left and follow it through the tunnel and all the way to Rodeo
Beach.*

Red Rocks Beach

One of the best. Not nearly as spectacular as Edun Cove to the south,
but it has lots of sand, sun and a more intimate feeling than any of the
other beaches. Red Rocks is also the only nude beach where it's
reasonably safe to body surf or swim. At low tide you can walk over
from the south end of Stinson Beach, but at high tide the beaches are
separate.

*To Get There: Head north across the Golden Gate Bridge and take the
Mill Valley/Stinson Beach exit. Take a left at the first stoplight onto*

Highway 1; follow the signs from there to Stinson Beach. Just before you get to the parking area for Red Rocks Beach, you'll be able to see the long, white beach of Stinson about a mile ahead. You'll then come onto the two parking lots on either side of the road. They're usually crowded on a nice day. The path down to the beach is near a metal gate in the parking lot on the west side of the road. Watch your step.

80 SEE ONE OF THE SEVEN ENGINEERING WONDERS OF THE WORLD

Even drive on it. It's the "other bridge" out there in the Bay, the San Francisco-Oakland Bay Bridge. Ever since it was completed in 1936, it has had to stand in the shadow of its more famous golden sister, even though the Bay Bridge is twice as long, cost twice as much to build and carries over twice the traffic load of the Golden Gate Bridge. The reason, of course, is one of style. The Golden Gate Bridge took nature and improved on it. The Bay Bridge bullied nature around.

The Bay Bridge starts out from Oakland as an awkward cantilever-style bridge, bores straight through Yerba Buena Island in a giant, four-story hole and then reaches across to San Francisco in two graceful suspension spans (for a grand total of three bridges and one hole). But that's not the reason why the Bay Bridge is considered one of the seven engineering wonders of the world. The reason is the monstrous concrete island that roots the San Francisco side of the bridge to the Bay floor. This cement island is actually bigger than the Great Pyramid and took more concrete to pour than the Empire State Building. We're talking big. Unfortunately, the Bay Bridge is almost no fun to drive. Better you should just step back, admire one of the seven engineering wonders of the world, and move on.

81 Take the Best Boat Ride on the Bay

It's the San Francisco-Larkspur ferry, hands down. Don't even think of it as a commuter ferry. Think of it instead as a posh nightclub with water wings. Sidle up to one of the bars or nestle into the comfortable cocktail seating and enjoy the good life in San Francisco. The leisurely trip takes you right past Alcatraz, gives you a postcard view of the Golden Gate Bridge and comes about as close to San Quentin as is possible without a sentence. Mind you, there isn't much to do once you get to the Larkspur terminal, but the trip is still well worth it.

The San Francisco-Larkspur ferry runs seven days a week. The ride takes about 40 minutes each way and costs about $3 round trip. If you miss the two commute periods, you'll have the sleek, gas turbine vessel practically to yourself. It loads from behind the Ferry Building, near the Embarcadero Center. To get there, take BART or the California cable car line to their Embarcadero stops. Phone 332-6600 for schedule information.

82 See a Ship Off

Now here's something that you don't get to do every day: tour a mammoth, ocean-bound liner. Fact is, very few San Franciscans get the chance anymore, so badly has our status as a center of shipping been lately slipping. But during the summer months, a couple of passenger ships still pass through San Francisco on a regular basis. You're usually welcome to tour these ships just before they put out to sea again. Both of San Francisco's daily newspapers list ship arrivals and departures (as anyone who has read *The Maltese Falcon* well knows). A better idea, however, is to call the individual lines listed below to find out when they'll have a ship in port.

Prudential Lines
Prudential has at least one ship in San Francisco each week during the year. An hour is set aside during freight unloading for visitors to board. Phone 777-8200.

Princess Cruises
Princess has ships in port during the summer months only. Public visiting is allowed two-and-one-half hours before sailing. Phone 362-8600.

Royal Viking
Ships in port throughout the year. Pick up boarding passes at the Royal Viking offices in the Embarcadero Center or at the gangway. Phone 398-8000.

Sitmar
Sitmar has ships in San Francisco during the summer months only. Passes are handed out at the gangway. Phone 788-7616.

83 Picnic in the Middle of the Bay

Angel Island, the largest of the islands in the San Francisco Bay, is also the most fun. Like the other islands—Alcatraz, Treasure and Yerba Buena—Angel Island has spent most of its history as a military installation. Beginning in the mid-1950s, however, Angel Island has been gradually deeded back to the people. Today, just about the entire one square mile of sun-drenched island is available to the public for hiking, biking, sun bathing or just some creative picture taking. An asphalt road circles the island, and several well-mapped trails lead you up and down the lush hills. If you're understandably tired of climbing hills, you can hop an open-air tram for a one-hour narrated tour of the island.

If it all sounds like a great picnic spot, it is. There's a full-service picnic area in Ayala Cove (near the ferry dockings), as well as a thousand places to set down along the trails. If you didn't bring any picnic fixings with you, check #100 for charming rent-a-picnics.

Harbor Carriers operates a commercial ferry to and from the island via Tiburon, an artsy village on the Marin side of the Bay. Between Memorial and Labor Days, four boats leave daily from 10 a.m.-3:45 p.m. During the rest of the year, the boats sail on weekends and holidays, only. The boats sail from Pier 43, on Fisherman's Wharf. Phone 546-2815. Admission.

The tram tour of the island runs daily from Memorial to Labor Days, and weekends only from April to October. Phone 435-1915. Admission.

84 VISIT A REAL-LIVE TREASURE ISLAND

Treasure Island, a four hundred-acre, man-made appendage to Yerba Buena Island, is one of the true architectural achievements of San Francisco, ranking alongside the Golden Gate Bridge and the Transamerica Pyramid. It's not as famous, of course, nor nearly as noticeable. That's because it (a) lies flat to the water and is hard to see, (b) is a military base these days and doesn't really court attention, and (c) is something San Francisco would just as soon forget.

Treasure Island was built as the third part of San Francisco's 1930s Trinity. The Golden Gate Bridge and the Bay Bridge were completed within six months of each other in 1936. Treasure Island was added to the Bay for their coming-out party, the 1939-40 Golden Gate International Exposition. The WPA picked up the tab, and San Francisco figured to pick up an airport. Yup, right out there in front of God and everybody.

Things didn't work out quite like they were planned. The party was a bust—in part because New York was also having a world's fair, but mostly because the U.S. was about to go to war and fun had gone out of style. And Treasure Island was quickly found to be too small, too close to the two bridges and too close to Oakland—no small point of pride—to suit San Francisco as an airport. Considerable face was saved when the Navy traded San Francisco's present airport site even up for Treasure Island.

Treasure Island remained closed to the public until 1976, when a museum and mural were opened in the main administration building (built originally as the headquarters for Pan Am Airlines). The mural, depicting the Navy and Marine Corps in the Pacific, is purported to be the largest in America. The museum, which was intended only as a Bicentennial gesture, has since been given an indefinite lease on life. The museum is of frankly marginal interest, unless you run into the semi-annual Golden Gate Exposition retrospective, which, among other things, details how the island was built. The trip out is almost worth it just for the spectacular view back to San Francisco.

To get to Treasure Island, simply take the Bay Bridge to the "Treasure Island" exit. The museum is housed in the first major building on the island. It's open seven days a week, 10 a.m.-3:30 p.m. Phone 765-6182. Free.

SAUSALITO

SAUSALITO

Of all the communities ringing the San Francisco Bay, only Sausalito has successfully cut itself in on San Francisco's tourist bonanza. The metamorphosis of the once-sleepy little town bordering on the Bay into a timeless seaside village came about quickly and completely during the 1960s. The boom was brought on by Sausalito's spreading reputation as a quaint artist's community, and by its strategic location: (a) on a sightline to San Francisco; and (b) on the way to popular Muir Woods. Specifically, it was the weekend gatherings in Sausalito of tourists on their way to or from Muir Woods that first alerted a couple of enterprising businessmen to the town's commercial potential. In 1962, they converted an old parking garage on Bridgeway (the main street of Sausalito) into a multi-floor shopping bazaar called the Village Fair. This prompted rents along the street to rise and resident-oriented businesses to leave, initiating a furious take-over by the boutiques, galleries and restaurants that now crowd the street. In 1970, ferry service was restored to Sausalito after a twenty-nine-year hiatus, cinching a year-round tourist trade.

Rapid change is nothing new to Sausalito, however. It was a wide-open gambling town back in the early 1900s, affectionately known as the "Monte Carlo of the West." The main stretch of Bridgeway was crowded with bordellos, saloons and gambling dens, all of which were swept away by a wave of propriety that washed over Sausalito shortly after the enfranchisement of women. During Prohibition, however, Sausalito's harbor became a depot for rum runners, who waited outside the Golden Gate Strait until a heavy fog allowed them to slip anonymously into the harbor, past Federal inspectors.

Sausalito had slid into the grips of normalcy when World War II brought a rash of heavy industry to Marin and new residents to town, many of whom stayed on after the war. It was then, too, that a post-war generation of artists began to arrive, attracted by the aesthetics and economics of the still-quiet town. Long-time residents complain that it is exactly those two qualities that have been swept away in Sausalito's precipitous rush to become an Attraction. For your own purposes, however, you'll still find Sausalito to be sunny, Mediterranean and funky-but-chic. Plan on at least half a day and one full meal while there. Try also to take the ferry over. It's the cheapest boat ride on the Bay, and the best way going. Phone 332-6600 for schedule information.

Here are a few other things to look for in Sausalito:

85 Visit a Restaurant of Ill Repute

At the south end of Sausalito, just as Bridgeway veers to the right and heads up a hill, you'll come to a boardwalk. The first house you pass on the boardwalk is the Jack London House. London lived in the double-turreted house at the turn of the century, when it was a combination beer garden and rooming house. London is believed to have written *The Sea Wolf* there.

However, there's an even more famous house at the end of the boardwalk. It's Sally Stanford's Valhalla restaurant, the oldest continuing business in Sausalito, dating back to the 1850s. Now Miss Stanford knows a thing or two about long-lived professions, being one of the most famous of the world's oldest. (Dyan Cannon played Stanford in a TV adaptation of her autobiographical *Lady of the House*.) Sally has also turned a stint or two as mayor of Sausalito. Her picturesque restaurant is done up to resemble—what else—a bordello, right down to red lights in the window. It's a great place to catch a drink or a meal before you turn back to downtown Sausalito.

86 SEE THE SEMI-FAMOUS SAUSALITO SEAL

At the start of your short stroll toward Sally Stanford's are a couple of minor curiosities. The first is just past the Trident restaurant on Bridgeway Avenue: a cute little bronze seal, alternately sunning itself or up on its rocks in high tide. The Sausalito Seal was placed at the edge of the Bay in 1957 by an artist who simply enjoyed watching the seals off the shoreline. (If you listen carefully, you might even be able to hear them.) The original seal was concrete, but had to be replaced by the present bronze version in 1966.

87 *SEE THE GREAT WALL OF SAUSALITO*

You've heard of San Simeon, William Randolph Hearst's monumental and unfinished castle down the California coast, yes? Well, Hearst originally intended to build San Simeon on a Sausalito hill overlooking the San Francisco Bay, but when Hearst threw up a huge support wall some six hundred feet long and ninety feet high to anchor his dream home, Sausalito was outraged. The townspeople rose *en masse* to oppose the publishing magnate, and may well have forced Hearst to build elsewhere if Hearst hadn't first decided to build elsewhere anyway. San Simeon was eventually built on an ocean outpost halfway between San Francisco and Los Angeles.

To see Hearst's incredible tall wall, stand directly in front of the Sausalito Seal on Bridgeway Avenue. Now pivot 180 degrees. You'll see the wall halfway up the hill on the other side of Bridgeway.

88 Take the Super "No Frills" Tour of San Francisco

The quickest and easiest way to get above it all is to head out to an old warehouse at the north end of Sausalito. There you'll find an unlikely two-acre recreation of the entire San Francisco/Bay Area region, complete with a miniature Alcatraz and Golden Gate Bridge. If you're lucky enough to be there when the tide movement of the San Francisco Bay is being charted, you'll even get to see the whole Bay flushed out into the mock-Pacific in a mere eight minutes. Not bad, considering it takes God and nature four hours to turn the same trick.

The Bay Model is a science project funded by the U.S. Army Corps of Engineers in 1957 to study man's impact on the fragile Bay ecosystem. Recently, the model has been opened to the public for interesting and educational self-tours. It's also a great way to get a grasp of the Bay Area. Imagine yourself as tall as the Transamerica Pyramid, able to leap great cities in a single bound. Superman ain't got nothing on you.

The Bay Model is in a former shipyard at the north end of Sausalito. A taxi from downtown Sausalito will cost you about $2. It's open Mon.-Fri. 9 a.m.-4 p.m., and on selected Saturdays. Phone 332-3871 to find out if they'll be running the water in the Bay. Free.

89 *SEE A REDWOOD THAT ISN'T YOUR NEIGHBOR'S PICNIC TABLE*

Finally, Sausalito is a good jumping off point for Muir Woods, the community of tall trees that brought about the influx of big bucks into

Sausalito in the first place. Muir Woods is all that remains of the vast redwood forests that used to surround San Francisco. Those trees that you don't see today were felled to help build San Francisco. The redwoods of Muir Woods were spared because they were relatively inaccessible. That would hardly have been hedge enough following the Great Earthquake of 1906. Fortunately, however, the land had come into private hands the year before the holocaust. It was then deeded to the U.S. Government, which declared it a National Monument in 1908 and named it in honor of John Muir, naturalist and the first president of the Sierra Club.

There are six miles of paths through Muir Woods, connecting with trails that lead to the ocean and the top of Mt. Tamalpais. The easiest trails take twenty to thirty minutes to circle back to the beginning. A longer loop takes about one-and-one-half hours. You can pick up a booklet along the trail that will alert you to the silent symphony being played before your senses.

There are several ways to get to Muir Woods. Gray Line runs tours out of San Francisco, as do most of the charter tour agencies listed in the yellow pages. A taxi from Sausalito will run you about $20 for a one-and-one-half hour round trip. You can also go by Golden Gate Transit bus from San Francisco or Sausalito—Phone 332-6600 for information. The park is open seven days a week from 8 a.m. to sunset, but the early morning hours are generally the most peaceful and least crowded. It's always cool in the woods, so bring along a jacket or sweater. Phone 338-2595. Admission.

SPOT TOURS

90 GOT THE WILL BUT DON'T KNOW THE WAY?

Following is a list of the tour operators and guided tours available in San Francisco.

Gray Line

Gray Line has a rather cozy arrangement with the Public Utilities Commission, whereby they're the only motor carrier in San Francisco allowed to handle passengers on a per capita basis. The break for you is that the PUC sets the rates and keeps them reasonable. The disadvantage is that you travel in huge buses and stop only in places that are able to process a large number of people, meaning that you won't get into the more interesting nooks and crannies. You can do a lot better with a good pair of walking shoes and this book (well, you didn't expect complete objectivity, did you?).

Gray Line offers a range of tours of San Francisco and the surrounding area. The tours are detailed in their free brochures, available in most hotel and motel lobbies. Most of the tours are offered year round, although the schedules do vary with the season. Gray Line also provides pickup and delivery service from most of the hotels in San Francisco. Phone 771-4000.

Chinese Heritage Walk

The Chinese Culture Foundation offers an interesting tour of Chinatown every Saturday at 2 p.m. The guides are Chinatown residents, which means they're knowledgeable and often quite political. They'll also take you places in Chinatown where you wouldn't be allowed on your own. The tours leave from the Chinatown Holiday Inn, 750 Kearny Street (across from Portsmouth Plaza). Phone 986-1822 for reservations. There is a fee.

Ding How Tours

Ding How conducts a two-and-one-half hour evening tour of China-town. You can also include a meal in a Chinatown restaurant, at an additional charge. You're delivered to Chinatown by taxi and hoof it the rest of the way. Ding How Tours is at 115 Waverly Place, in the heart of Chinatown. Phone 981-8399 for reservations. Fee.

JJ Walking Tours

This is the best tour if you want to get a feel for the streets of San Francisco. "JJ" and her guides give tours of the Jackson Square area, North Beach, Japantown and Union Street; but her best tour by far is Chinatown. She's become a trusted friend of the community over the years and can go places other outsiders can't. "JJ's" tour lasts about two hours (three, if you include lunch). The tours go out daily between 10:30 a.m. and 1:30 p.m., but the hours and tours are flexible. Phone 441-8270 for reservations, 24 hours. Fee.

Mission District Mural Tour

A one-hour tour of the sites of the colorful and intricate Mission District murals. The tour is given the second Saturday of each month, and leaves from the Mexican Museum, 1855 Folsom Street, in the Mission District. Phone 621-1224. Fee. You can also pick up a map at the museum for a self-guided tour.

Following is a variety of museums and businesses that offer guided tours of their premises:

Alcatraz

The National Park Service offers free tours of "the Rock" daily, though you do have to pay for the boat ride out. The tours leave from Pier 43 on Fisherman's Wharf. Phone 546-2805 for reservations. (See #5).

Anchor Steam Brewery

The Anchor Steam Brewery doesn't really encourage tours, truth to tell, but you can wrangle one if you're something of a student of the art of brewing. Phone 863-1495 for reservations. (See #20).

Angel Island

You can take a one-hour narrated tram tour of the island daily during the summer and weekends during the winter. Both the tram and the boat ride out will cost you. The boats leave from Pier 43, on Fisherman's Wharf. Phone 546-2815 for reservations. (See #83).

Arboretum

Sixty acres of botanical splendors in Golden Gate Park. Tours given daily at noon. Phone 921-9784. Free. (See #77).

The Bed and Breakfast Inn

A charming, European-style hotel just off Union Street. Tours given daily at noon. Phone 921-9784. Free.

California Historical Society

A perfectly maintained Victorian mansion serves as the showcase for a variety of paintings and artifacts from San Francisco's history. Located in the Pacific Heights district at 2090 Jackson Street. Tours are given Wednesday, Saturday and Sunday from 1 p.m. to 5 p.m. Phone 567-1848. Tours free with admission.

California Palace of the Legion of Honor

The French collection displayed within this art museum is excellent. The view, overlooking the Pacific, is dazzling. Tours are given daily at 2 p.m. Located on the western edge of the City. Phone 558-2881 for directions. Tours free with admission. (See #45).

Civic Center/City Hall

This tour takes you through San Francisco's grand City Hall and aging Civic Center. The tours begin in the San Francisco Library, 200 Larkin Street. They're given Thursdays at noon and Saturdays at 10 a.m. Phone 558-3949. Free.

M. H. deYoung Museum and Asian Art Museum of San Francisco

Two serious collections of art and artifacts housed in the same building in Golden Gate Park. One admission gets you into both. Tours are given daily between 1 p.m. and 2 p.m. Phone 752-5561. Tours free with admission. (See #44).

Fireman's Pioneer Museum

A surprise, guaranteed to bring out the kid in anyone. There's a lot of fire equipment, hats and uniforms dating back to the Gold Rush, as well as a couple of classy horse-drawn fire wagons. Located in Fire Station Number 10, 655 Presidio Avenue (at Pine Street). Volunteer tour guides are on duty Thursday through Sunday from 1 p.m. to 4 p.m. Phone 558-3949. Free.

Fort Point

The last brick fort built in the U.S., and the only one ever built west of the Mississippi. Located underneath the Golden Gate Bridge. Tours given weekdays every hour on the hour, weekends every half hour. Phone 556-1693. Free. (See #36).

Grace Cathedral

The largest church building in the West and rather awe-inspiring inside, if you're into such things. Grace Cathedral took fifty-four years to build from cornerstone to consecration. It's located on Nob Hill at California and Taylor Streets, on the California cable car line. Phone 776-6611 for reservations. Free.

Haas Lilienthal House

A well-preserved Victorian providing a glimpse of the good life in San Francisco before the Earthquake. Open Wednesdays and Sundays only. Located at 2007 Franklin Street. The only way to go through the house is by tour. Phone 441-3004. Admission.

Mexican Museum

Not so much a museum as a gallery displaying all manner of Mexican art from the past to the present. Located at 1855 Folsom Street, in the Mission District. Tours given Tuesday through Friday from 10 a.m-5 p.m. Phone 621-1224. Admission.

The Old Mint

Simply the best historical museum in San Francisco. Located at Fifth and Mission Streets, downtown. Tours given every hour on the hour between 10 a.m. and 4 p.m. Closed Sunday and Monday. Phone 556-3630. Free. (See #34.)

San Francisco Museum of Modern Art

The only museum in the West devoted exclusively to twentieth century art. A great place to spend a rainy afternoon. Located at Van Ness Avenue and McAllister Street, near City Hall. Tours given Tuesday through Sunday at 1:15 p.m. Phone 863-8800. Tours free with admission. (See #43.)

Wine Museum of San Francisco

The grape in all its glory. Located at 633 Beach Street, in Fisherman's Wharf. Tours given daily between 2 p.m. and 4 p.m. Phone 673-6990. Free. (See #51.)

91 TAKE A TIP-TOP TOUR OF SAN FRANCISCO

One of the best things to do in San Francisco is simply nothing at all. Slip into an elevator, slide up to one of San Francisco's skyline saloons, settle in over a potted spirit and simply soak up the view. On a clear day, San Francisco stretches out before you like a vintage Willie McCovey pulling in a short throw at first. By night, the City shifts and shimmers like a socialite in a sequinned dress.

San Francisco's magnificent aerial view comes in all directions and dimensions with all manner of diversions. All of the rooftop lounges are located within just a few blocks of each other in the Downtown/Nob Hill/Financial District area, and all are within a block of the cable car lines. Here's where to enjoy the view:

Top of the Mark

The granddaddy of them all. The Top of the Mark invented the rooftop view of San Francisco and is, if not quite the Must that it once was, at least a Should. The Top of the Mark is on the 19th floor of the fabled Mark Hopkins Hotel, California and Mason Streets, Nob Hill. Open seven days a week, 10:30 a.m.-1:30 a.m. No entertainment. Buffet luncheon, no dinners. No cover, no minimum. Phone 392-3434.

Carnelian Room

The reigning heavyweight. Perched atop the Bank of America Building, the Carnelian Room is as high as you can go in San Francisco. Unfortunately, it also tends to lay San Francisco's sensuous curves out flat like a map. The Carnelian Room is on the fifty-second floor of the Bank of America building, California Street between Montgomery and Kearny Streets. Open seven days a week until at least 10:30 p.m. No entertainment. Dinner, Sunday Brunch. No cover, no minimum. Phone 433-7500.

Equinox

Not too high and not all that much of a view, but the Equinox compensates with a revolving bar. Don't set anything on the window sill, however, or you won't see it for 45 minutes. Equinox is on the twentieth floor of the Hyatt Regency Hotel, at the base of California Street in the Embarcadero Center. Open seven days a week, 11 a.m.-2 a.m. No entertainment. Lunch, dinner. No cover, no minimum. Phone 788-1234.

Sherlock Holmes Public Pub

A view of the City and a glimpse of Sherlock Holmes' famous 221 B Baker Street sitting room. Who would figure it smack dab in the middle of downtown San Francisco? The Sherlock Holmes Public Pub is on the thirtieth floor of the Holiday Inn Union Square, Powell and Sutter Streets. Open seven days a week, noon till at least 11 p.m. Cocktail piano and guitar. No food. No cover, no minimum. Phone 398-8900. (See #69.)

Reflections and One Up

Adjacent bars with a chrome and glass ambience. Reflections and One Up are on the thirty-sixth floor of the Hyatt on Union Square, Stockton Street between Post and Sutter Streets. One Up is open seven days a week, 5 p.m.-1:30 a.m. Reflections keeps the same hours but is closed Sunday and Monday. One Up is a piano bar. Reflections features a jazz vocalist and dancing. No food in either, although there is an adjacent restaurant. No cover, no minimum. Phone 398-1234.

Fairmont Crown Room

The Fairmont Crown Room probably has the best view of San Francisco in the City. Unfortunately, the bar itself looks like a shopping center smorgasbord restaurant and doesn't even come close to getting it on Nob Hill. The Fairmont Crown Room is on the twenty-fourth floor of the Fairmont Hotel, California and Mason Streets, Nob Hill. Open seven days a week until 1:30 a.m. No entertainment. Buffet dinner. No cover, no minimum. Phone 772-5131.

92 GET A BIRD'S EYE VIEW OF SAN FRANCISCO

San Francisco is a very compact and succinct city. Really. Now you might find that a little hard to swallow if you've just spent the day climbing hills and chasing cable cars, but if you could see the City from the air you'd appreciate just how small San Francisco really is.

Here are two places that'll take you up on it:

Commodore Helicopters

Commodore is the easiest to get to. It's right down on Fisherman's Wharf at Pier 43, next to the Alcatraz tours. A four-minute spin over Fisherman's Wharf will cost you $6 (half that if you're a kid ten or under). Commodore flies seven days a week between 10 a.m. and sunset, weather permitting. Phone 981-4832.

Helicoptours

Helicoptours offers five different flights, from a five-minute, $8 quickie to a thirty-minute, $48 comprehensive tour of San Francisco. If you have a specific tour in mind they'll even cut you a special deal. They're at Pier 46. (Note: Despite its apparent proximity to Fisherman's Wharf, Pier 46 is actually several miles away since all even-numbered piers are south of the Ferry Building, all odd-numbered piers north.) Phone 621-5900.

93 THE OTHER GUIDE TO SAN FRANCISCO's GUIDE TO THE OTHER SAN FRANCISCO

Seven little secrets San Francisco would just as soon keep to itself.

San Quentin

You know, of course, of Alcatraz, San Franicsco's celebrated "Rock." You may not know that another infamous prison—San Quentin—lies just twelve miles north of Alcatraz on the banks of the Bay. San Quentin is California's oldest prison. It first closed its doors for business in 1852, necessitated by the lawless lot that were just then finding their way back to San Francisco after the first flush of the Gold Rush. Over the years, the "Q" has kept such cons as Black Bart (see #70), Sirhan Sirhan, Charles Manson, William Harris, and George Jackson, who was shot and killed at San Quentin in 1971.

The easiest way to get to San Quentin short of a sentence is to take the Larkspur ferry from San Francisco, which will dock you within rifle range of the prison. There's a small gift shop at the prison entrance featuring inmate handiwork. For information, phone 454-1460.

Room 1219, St. Francis Hotel

On Labor Day weekend, 1921, silent film star Roscoe "Fatty" Arbuckle gathered up a few of his Hollywood cronies, drove up to San Francisco and set about celebrating his fat new $3 million movie contract. As a result of that drunken weekend, one woman died, Fatty was charged with murder, and Hollywood was rocked by its first full-blown scandal.

Exactly what happened that weekend in Room 1219 of the St. Francis Hotel will never be known. This much is: Twenty-one-year old Virginia Rappe was carried unconscious from 1219 and died several days later of massive internal injuries. In court, Fatty's "million dollar defense team" charged that Rappe's death was due to a botched abortion attempt, the money for which she was trying to extort from Fatty in Room 1219.

The prosecution charged that Fatty had sexually abused Virginia Rappe. They produced several witnesses who claimed to hear Fatty leer as he and Rappe entered 1219: "This is the chance I've waited for for a long time."

It took three trials, but Fatty Arbuckle was finally judged innocent of any crime. The final jury even went so far as to declare: "Acquittal is not enough for Roscoe Arbuckle. We feel that a great injustice has been done him." The greater injustice was about to begin. Fatty's movies were banned from the screen in a baby-with-the-bathwater attempt of atonement by Hollywood. His career washed up, Fatty Arbuckle died a broken man in 1933.

You can still rent Room 1219, for a mere $73 a night, double occupancy. Phone the St. Francis Hotel at 397-7000 for information and reservations.

Billie Holiday Suite

Although Mark Twain never set foot in the Mark Twain Hotel, Billie Holiday did. She was there the night of 22 January 1949 when police broke in and busted Billie and her husband for possession of opium. Billie maintained her innocence and was acquitted. The rooms she was busted in have since been done over in the style of the day and canonized the Billie Holiday Suite. You can rent the rooms (impeccably furnished, right down to the 1949 newspaper clippings of her bust), or call the Mark Twain Hotel to arrange for a tour of the modest suite. The Mark Twain Hotel is at 345 Taylor Street, two blocks west of Union Square. Phone 673-2332.

Charles Manson House

In the spring of 1967, Charles Manson joined the mass migration of flower children into San Francisco's Haight Ashbury. Except that Charles Manson was hardly a flower child. He was thirty-two-years old. He had spent seventeen years—more than half of his life—behind bars. He had a prison-slick rap and enough of an acquaintance with Scientology and Dale Carnegie techniques to pass himself off as a lower order guru on impressionable young girls. Several months later, when Charles Manson pulled out of San Francisco in an old school bus, he had managed to enlist Susan Atkins, Squeaky Fromme, Mary Brunner, and Patricia Krenwinkle in his "Family." Over the next two years, the Manson Family would be responsible for an estimated thirty-five murders, including the famous Tate-LaBianca killings.

Charles Manson's house in the Haight is at 636 Cole Street, half a block off of Haight Street.

Altamont

In rock mythology, Altamont is where the Woodstock dream of peace, love and music died, beneath the sinister spell of the Rolling Stones and at the drunken hand of the Hell's Angels. The Stones, it was whispered, orchestrated the killing of eighteen-year-old Meredith Hunter in front of the stage for the convenience of their concert movie, "Gimme Shelter." The Hell's Angels agreed to police the concert in return for a few hundred dollars' worth of beer and seemingly all the hippies they could pummel. Altamont did in fact go very badly, but for very good reason. It was to be a final, free celebration climaxing the 1969 Stones American tour. When the group was denied a permit for Golden Gate Park, they settled on Sears Point Raceway in Marin County. At the last minute the parent company of the race track demanded a cut of any film shot there, and the Stones balked. With half a million concert-goers bearing down hard, concert organizers struck an eleventh-hour deal for Altamont Raceway in Alameda County, east of San Francisco. An armada of helicopters was rounded up to perform the miraculous task of creating a concert site from scratch in two days, and the show came off—with its celebrated hitches—on 7 December 1969.

Altamont Raceway is located in a lonely corner of Alameda County, some sixty-five miles from San Francisco. It's no longer in use, and has deteriorated into a windswept ruin of the Aquarian Age. To get to Altamont, take the Bay Bridge out of San Francisco to Interstate 580 East. Go past Livermore, over the Altamont Pass to the Byron Road exit. Take Byron Road under the freeway until you pass the raceway.

People's Temple

For two weeks in November of 1978, the world stood dumbfounded by two tragedies that cast a dark and incriminating shadow on San Francisco. The City was just coming to grips with its grief and personal loss in the People's Temple mass suicides when Dan White walked into San Francisco City Hall and killed Mayor George Moscone and Supervisor Harvey Milk. Initially, there was some paranoid speculation that the two tragedies might somehow be related, since People's Temple leader Jim Jones was a political appointee and sometime ally of Moscone. There was no connection.

Jim Jones was a social crusader who lost his way in the jungles of Guyana. He founded his integrated People's Temple in Indianapolis, but picked up momentum when he moved to a church in San Francisco's black Fillmore district in 1971. He shrewdly endeared himself to local and national politicians by turning Temple members out in wholesale numbers for political events. In 1975, Mayor Moscone rewarded Jones with a position as Chairman of the Housing Authority. Shortly thereafter, the dark underside of Jones' personality and operations surfaced in a magazine article. Jones may well have been prosecuted if he'd stuck around for publication of the article. He didn't. Using his political contacts, Jones fled to his commune in Guyana and left San Francisco in the summer of 1977, his flock in tow.

In the aftermath of the People's Temple horror, many questioned why so many urban blacks would follow a white man to the jungles of South America. The best answer came from a Fillmore resident who gestured to the surrounding ghetto and said: "Just look around. There sure wasn't anything keeping them here."

You'll find the old People's Temple Building at 1859 Geary Street, between Steiner and Fillmore Streets. The building was sold in a 1979 public auction to the Korean Presbyterian Church.

Hot Potato

On 27 November 1978, deposed San Francisco Supervisor Dan White crawled through a window in City Hall to avoid passing a metal detector, then shot and killed Mayor George Moscone and Supervisor Harvey Milk. The senseless murders were precipitated by White's resignation from the Board of Supervisors. White gave up the $9000-a-year job citing the financial and mental strain of tending to the City, his family and his French fry stand on Pier 39. When White's family subsequently offered to help him out financially, White asked for the job back. Feeling that Moscone reneged on a promised reinstatement, White went looking for the Mayor. The course of events that White set in motion that day extracted a horrible payment in suffering from the people of San Francisco. White himself was sentenced to only a total of seven years and eight months in prison for the double murders.

The White family's French fry stand has been renamed The Potato Place. It's in an all-purpose eatery called The Galley, just inside the entrance to Pier 39 on Fisherman's Wharf.

94 ROCK AROUND THE CLOCK

If you're in town for a couple of nights, then you're in for some fun, because San Francisco gets down when the sun does. If you like jazz, you can see some of the legends of jazz most any night at the Keystone Korner in North Beach. The Fairmont Venetian Room on Nob Hill headlines various Vegas-types. There's usually a Broadway road show or two at either the Curran or the Orpheum and some excellent repertory theatre at the Geary Theatre downtown. You'll find first-rate symphony, ballet and opera in season and just about anything you could possibly want on Broadway in North Beach.

And you can get your rocks off, any night of the week at most any hour. To prove it, here's an outline for a non-stop rock n roll weekend, from 6 p.m. Friday to 6 p.m. Sunday. Bop till you drop.

Friday Night

6 p.m.: You'll need your strength for the weekend, so start quietly with a meditative meal at Carlos Santana's excellent vegetarian restaurant, Dipti Nivas, 216 Church Street. *8 p.m.*: Now comes the hard part: picking from the wealth of prime time activities. The Old Waldorf, Boarding House and Great American Music Hall all book top name club bands, and Bill Graham usually has a show in town. Pick up a copy of the Friday *San Francisco Examiner*, which sorts out the weekend in its TGIF section. *10 p.m.*: Strut your stuff over to The City, San Francisco's posh and boss New Wave discotheque, 936 Montgomery. *Midnight*: Put on your party hat and join the unconventional conventioneers at the Rocky Horror Picture Show at the Strand Theatre, 1127 Market Street.

Saturday Morning

2 a.m.: Only one person can top *Rocky Horror*: Edsel Ford Fung, the world's rudest waiter (#58) at Sam Wo's, a jook and jive joint in Chinatown at 813 Washington Street. *3 a.m.*: Try your luck at a little all night pool at Palace Billards, 949 Market Street. *5 a.m.*: If you're beginning to droop, the bright lights and all night crazies at Cala Foods, California and Hyde Streets, will snap you back to reality. *6 a.m.*: If that didn't wake you, try the fresh air at Fisherman's Wharf, where the fishing fleets are just pulling out of harbor. Then head over to the nearby Eagle Cafe in Pier 39 for a hale and hearty breakfast. *7 a.m.*: There's not much shakin' now, so do a little rock hunting in the Mission District. A block and a half off Mission Street on 15th is Ramona Street, which so inspired the Ramones when they were in town that they named one of their songs after it. At 189 Precita Avenue, just off Mission, is the Beatle House, famous for its outside motif. *8 a.m.*: Now get onto 101 heading south. You'll quickly pass the 280 turn-off, which passes the rows of track houses that inspired Malvena Reynold's "Little Boxes." Pete Seeger had the shortest hit in the history of Top 40 with the song. Turn around at Candlestick Park, the site of the last Beatles concert ever on 29 August 1966. *9 a.m.*: Opening time at Perry's, 1944 Union Street, and not a minute too soon. Perry's makes the best Bloody Mary in town. *10 a.m.*: Step back in time to 1949 in the Billie Holiday Suite at the Mark Twain Hotel, 345 Taylor Street (#93). *11 a.m.*: What better to do on a Saturday morning than some shopping? Start in Fisherman's Wharf at Bill Graham's Rock Shop, 1333 Columbus Avenue (#28). Then walk up Columbus to Bay Street and Tower Records, San Francisco's largest and most complete record store. A couple of blocks farther up at 817 Columbus Avenue is Don Wehr's Music City, outfitters to every Bay Area band what am. *Noon*: Finally, head over to Supplies, 3128 16th Street, for the absolute latest in punk and cosmic funk.

Saturday Afternoon

1 p.m.: By now you're probably dead on your feet, so sit back and enjoy some music. Every Saturday afternoon at the Caffe Trieste, Vallejo and Grant in North Beach, the owner's family puts on an opera recital for their friends and customers. *3 p.m.*: When you tire of opera, beat your feet to the nearby Keystone Korner, 750 Vallejo, for their Saturday afternoon jam session. *5 p.m.*: Be nice to yourself. Head over to the Grand Central Sauna and Hot Tub Company, 15 Fell Street, for a wholesome tub and a rub (#98). *7 p.m.*: Eat to the beat at Hamburger Mary's, 1582 Folsom Street.

Saturday Night

8 p.m.: Prime time again. Check the papers to see what you missed last night. *10 p.m.*: Spend the rest of the evening in North Beach. Stop in first at City Lights Bookstore, 261 Columbus Avenue, famous repository of beatnik culture (#12). *11 p.m.*: Now get your fair share of abuse at the Fab Mab. The Mabuhay Gardens is San Francisco's first and best New Wave club. Just everybody makes the scene at the Mabuhay, 443 Broadway. *1 a.m.*: When you tire of making a scene of yourself, walk down the street to Enrico's, 504 Broadway, for a divinely decadent liqueur shake.

Sunday Morning

3 a.m.: If you think you just can't go on any longer, check into San Francisco's premiere rock hotel, The Miyako, Post and Laguna Streets. If you can, check out San Francisco's allegedly heterosexual bath house, the Sutro Bath House, 1015 Folsom Street. *9 a.m.*: With Sunday morning coming down, duck into Cecil Williams joyous Glide Memorial Church (#101), Ellis and Taylor Streets, for a tune and atonement. *11 a.m.*: Another tough decision: where to have brunch. You may want to choose the Garden Court at the Sheraton Palace, Market and New Montgomery Streets, where Nicolette Larson snapped the cover photo for her first album. Then again, you may not.

Sunday Afternoon

1 p.m.: All the action is in Golden Gate Park now. The best way to get around is to rent a pair of roller skates from one of the trucks that ring the park. *3 p.m.*: Since you're near the Haight Ashbury, make a pilgrimage to the old Dead House at 710 Ashbury Street and to the Airplane House at 2400 Fulton Street. Then trip over to Bill Graham's legendary Fillmore Auditorium, Fillmore and Geary Streets, and Winterland, just a couple of blocks away at Post and Steiner Streets. *5 p.m.*: Ride off into the sunset on a floating cocktail lounge, the Larkspur Ferry (#81). When you get back to San Francisco, Sunday night will be happening. Let it go on without you.

SPARE PARTS

95 THE TEN BEST SOUVENIRS OF SAN FRANCISCO

It's time for you to start thinking about what you're going to take back with you for the folks at home. Now you could let your duty slide until the last day and then duck into a hotel lobby for a cable car coin bank or one of those water-filled paperweights with the Golden Gate Bridge immersed in a snowstorm.

Or you could take the ten ideas below, embellish with a few of your own personal whims, and return home with a booty befitting the jewel of American cities and your own impeccable taste:

1. A Copy of "Howl" from City Lights Bookstore
Allen Ginsberg's *Howl* put City Lights on the map (see #12), but anything from Lawrence Ferlinghetti's hip bookstore makes for a great gift. (Be sure to get it in a City Lights bag.)

2. Irish Coffee glass from the Buena Vista
Irish Coffee is the granddaddy of coffee drinks (see #11), and an authentic BV glass will distinguish even the most tentative attempt. If you want to go a step further, pick up a bottle of the BV's personal brew, Tullamore Dew, in the nearby Cannery Gourmet Shop.

3. A special mint from the Old Mint
San Francisco is the only mint in the United States system that makes the commemorative proof sets of each year's coinage. The only way to purchase one of these special proof sets (double-struck, high-polish metal) is to put your name on a mailing list, which you can do at the Old Mint, Mission and Fifth Streets, downtown. The Old Mint also has for sale every commemorative medal ever struck by the government, as well as a lingering supply of 40 percent-silver Bicentennial sets.

4. Anchor Steam Beer memorabilia

The bottle makes a distinctive addition to any collection, and the T-shirt—available at the brewery and in discriminating gift shops—is one of the best shirts in town. (See #20.)

5. A Fillmore poster from Bill Graham's Rock Shop

Graham's shop is a find for the serious souvenir hound. Reproductions of Graham's original Fillmore posters top the list of collectibles here. (See #28.)

6. Ghirardelli Chocolate

But of course. You don't have to go to Ghirardelli Square to find San Francisco's own, home-churned chocolate, but it helps.

7. Sourdough starter

Could develop into a perpetual reminder of your stay-by-the-Bay.

8. The menu from John's Grill

During a tense scene in *The Maltese Falcon*, supersleuth Sam Spade stops off at John's Grill for an order of "chops, baked potato and sliced tomatoes." John's Grill commemorates Spade's novel excursion with a handsome menu cover, available for sale and suitable for framing. (See #14.)

9. Zap Comix

The underground comic flowered and reached full bloom during the heady days of the Haight Ashbury. Artists such as Spain Rodrigues, S. Clay Wilson and Victor Moscoso lived and worked in San Francisco. The most famous of all, however, was R. Crumb, who took up residence in the Haight and watched the stoned proceedings with amusement. Crumb's most famous work highlighted the most famous of all the underground comics, Zap Comix. There are nine different Zaps. The first two printings of Zap #1 go for as much as $150 these days (look for the printer's names—Plymell or Donahue—on the back cover), but you can pick up a new one for about a buck at any good comic book store. A good place to start is Golden Gate Comic Shop, 722 Columbus Avenue in North Beach. Phone 982-3511.

10. Postcard from the Postcard Palace

San Francisco isn't just another pretty place. So why bore the folks back home with just another postcard, when the Postcard Palace, 756 Columbus Avenue, stocks some only-in-San Francisco sentiments. For starters, there are various rock star cards, all snapped in San Francisco. There are postcards that proclaim "Greetings From San Francisco, The Saxophone Capital of the World," and maintain that "Whales Want Our Women." Or if you're trying to shake someone off your trail, you can send your greetings from Youngstown, Ohio, Syracuse, New York, or, of course, Anytown, USA. The Postcard Palace also carries some punk paraphernalia.

96 Dial An Event

If you'd like to schedule some area music, sports or theater into your day or evening, check out one of the various 24-hour activity lines or consult one of the newspaper activity calendars, listed below:

Dial-An-Event. 391-2000

The Convention and Visitors Bureau keeps this one up. Heavy on the major theater, civic, sports and free activities. There is one listing for Monday through Thursday, another to cover the weekend.

BASS Tickets. 835-3849

Includes everything that BASS (Bay Area Seating Service) sells tickets for, which is just about everything. By far the most complete listing of club, concert, sports and theater happenings, but it goes on forever. Have a pencil and paper handy.

KSAN Entertainment Line. 478-9600
Updated daily, this is the most current listing of club and concert activities.

KJAZ Live Jazz Line. 521-9336
A summary of area jazz appearances.

KYA Concert Connection. 478-3000
Lists major rock and jazz concert dates for the coming month.

KMEL Concert Connection. 397-0106
Covers club activity and major rock and jazz events.

KSFO Sports Dial. 478-9560
Gives sports results, major sports stories and a listing of upcoming games.

The Bay Guardian's "Day and Night"
A weekly tabloid, *The Bay Guardian*'s pull-out entertainment section is a thorough guide to the best entertainment bets for the coming week, with the emphasis on the inexpensive and offbeat. Available on the streets and at newsstands.

The San Francisco Examiner's "TGIF"
San Francisco's evening newspaper's "TGIF" guide is a spirited catalogue for the upcoming weekend, available in the Friday edition of the paper.

The San Francisco Chronicle's "Pink Section"
The distinctive pink supplement in the Sunday paper, AKA "Datebook." The Pink Section is the bible of Bay Area entertainment guides, and covers *everything* going on in San Francisco.

97 FIVE TIPS FOR THE HIP

Dressing for San Francisco

Understand that San Francisco is never *truly* warm. The average annual temperature is a cool 57° F. Even in San Francisco's warmest months—September and October—the average daily *high* is less than 70°. So do yourself a favor by dressing for warmth and comfort. Traditional lightweight summer clothing is seldom practical in San Francisco. A sweater or light topcoat is *de rigueur* for any outing in San Francisco and will get you through all but the coolest summer evenings and the winter months.

You'll also be doing a lot of walking in San Francisco. Be good to your dogs. Wear comfortable shoes or sneakers whenever and wherever possible. The hills in this town are tough enough without strapping on a pair of your own.

Driving in San Francisco

It's not nearly as tough as you might think. In fact, driving in San Francisco is a cinch compared to stopping in San Francisco. Forget your heart—it's your stomach that'll get left behind the first time you have to stop for a light halfway up one of San Francisco's slanted streets. And parking in this town is a rumor. Thank your lucky brake linings that San Francisco is small enough to walk. If you're not, here's a few rules of the road:

- If you're not practiced in the art of starting from a dead stop on a 30 percent incline, wave to the cars behind you to tell them to move back. Please.

- You may turn *right* on a red light in California after making a full stop.
- You may also turn *left* on a red light from a one-way street onto an intersecting one-way street, after stopping and providing it's not otherwise posted.
- When parking on a hill, you will be ticketed if you don't curb your wheels properly and distinctly. Turn your wheels to the left—into the street—when parking uphill. Turn them to the right—into the curb—when parking downhill. When in doubt, follow the lead of the cars in front of you.
- If you're ticketed with out-of-state plates, you will also get a notice warning you that your car can be impounded. Don't sweat it. In practice, the police won't worry about an out-of-state car until it has run up at least five parking tickets. Even at that, the tickets have to be issued in the same relative neighborhood so the police know where to come looking. Just be careful.
- Now then, you must remember this: DO NOT park between 7 and 9 a.m. and 4 and 6 p.m. in areas so posted. You will be ticketed *and* towed, for very good reason. Don't even chance it. Period.

Don't Call It "Frisco"

Time was when you'd drop a "Frisco" into a conversation and all eyes in the room would pivot and rivet you with such looks of contempt and hatred as to pucker your perma-presses. No one knows for sure when folks hereabouts started calling "Frisco" by its Christian name (the term was a popular one on the Barbary Coast), but San Francisco elder statesman Herb Caen fanned the flames of intolerance with these words in his 1953 book *Don't Call It Frisco* (Doubleday and Company):

Don't call it Frisco—it's SAN Francisco, because it was named after St. Francis of Assisi. And because "Frisco" is a nickname that reminds the city uncomfortably of the early, brawling, boister-

ous days of the Barbary Coast and the cribs and sailors who were shanghaied. And because "Frisco" shows disrespect for a city that is now big and proper and respectable. And because only tourists call it "Frisco," anyway, and you don't want to be taken for a tourist, do you?

Lately there's been a softening of the party line, at least on the part of Herb Caen, who in 1978 took one of his morning columns to explain that the admonition was:

A catch title, that's all. I was never sure about the reasoning behind the objection, even while voicing it. Other old-timers don't know either. They stumble around with words like "undignified" and "bawdy" and "coarse," as if there's something wrong with a city being any of those, which every city is. Maybe it has to do with San Francisco being "the city of St. Francis," and there is no St. Frisco. My recollection is that it's a waterfront-born nickname that the sailors used lovingly, back when this was the best (i.e., wildest) port of call in the Pacific.

And so maybe San Francisco is undergoing a change of heart. If so, there will probably be a long, long convalescence period. In the meantime, if you don't want to be taken for a tourist, well, don't call it "Frisco."

So What Do You Call It?

What, you may by now be wondering, does this place call itself, then? And what's all this stuff about the "Bay Area" and the "East Bay," anyway? Well, if you spend anytime in the area you'll quickly learn that the San Francisco-Oakland-San Jose region is a conglomerate of three major metropolises, each with its own suburbs, sports loyalties and bridge. To help you keep it straight, here's a quick translation of the local tongue:

Bay Area.

Used in general, it refers to the entire region surrounding the San Francisco Bay. More often, it's used by natives of San Francisco and Oakland to avoid saying the name of the other.

The City

Everybody agrees on one thing: San Francisco is "the City."

East Bay

The communities and counties surrounding Oakland and Berkeley on the east side of the Bay.

Golden State

How to say San Francisco, Oakland and San Jose without offending anyone? Diplomatically, as in "Golden State Warriors."

Marin County

Refers to the towns of wealthy and trendy Marin County to the north of San Francisco. Minus the "County," it refers to the experience. Marin County is less frequently referred to as:

North Bay

Too pedestrian.

Peninsula

Refers to the land south of San Francisco crowded on either side by the ocean and the Bay. At some point, San Francisco stops and San Jose starts, although no one is quite sure where anymore.

South Bay

The communities and counties surrounding San Jose. Actually, San Jose is still quite a ways from San Francisco both geographically and spiritually, although BART (Bay Area Rapid Transit) may eventually loop around the Bay and draw it into San Francisco's orbit. Or vice versa. No one is quite sure which anymore.

How To Ride A Cable Car

There are two sides to everything, including cable cars. Most passengers will simply flock to the side closest to them. Go immediately to the other side.

THE INSIDE COMPARTMENT

THE SEATS

THE LEAD POSITION

THE RUNNING BOARDS

The Inside Compartment
Fills up fast with namby-pambys, who also tend to congregate at the front of classrooms and the shallow end of the pool.

The Seats
Okay to use if the running boards are full. Generally, however, the seats should be left to elderly stroke victims who need a lot of sun but not much excitement.

The Running Boards
This is where God and Andrew Hallidie intended for you to ride a cable car.

The Lead Position

The best place on the cable car to ride. Since there are only two per trip, you may have to be thought pushy to get one. That's alright—you want your money's worth, don't you? Whoever assumes the lead position also assumes the attendant responsibility of waving to motorists and warning other passengers to keep their body parts in so they don't get them sheared off by passing cable cars.

98 IF THIS IS A HOT TUB THEN IT MUST BE SAN FRANCISCO

If you've made it through this much of San Francisco, then you're more than ready for two other turn-ons: The Grand Central Sauna and Hot Tub Company and Hot Tubs.

A word, first, from management: Grand Central and Hot Tubs are clean, wholesome, healthy places. Parties of up to four can rent a room equipped with a hot tub, a dry-heat sauna, a shower and a "resting place." If they sound like great places to soak your dogs, they are.

Being the consenting adult that you are, however, you should also know that the rooms are private, that the "resting place" by any other name is a bed and the one-to-three people that you can bring with you can be of any denomination and for any good reason—get it?

Grand Central and Hot Tubs are a hit, the first of their kind in the country. There's a natural juice bar at each to help you while away the wait, which can be upwards of an hour in the evening when all the rooms are filled (they don't take reservations). Things are usually mellower in the daytime.

The Grand Central Sauna and Hot Tub Company is at 15 Fell Street, near the Civic Center. It's open from Sunday through Thursday, 11 a.m. to midnight, Friday and Saturday 11 a.m. to 2 a.m. Phone 431-1370. Hot Tubs is at 2200 Van Ness Avenue, between Broadway and Vallejo Streets. It's open Sunday through Thursday, 11 a.m. to 1 a.m., Friday and Saturday, 11 a.m. to 2 a.m. Phone 441-8827.

99 Enjoy the Fruits of a Trip to the Wine Country (Without Really Going to the Wine Country)

If all your sampling of San Francisco's bounty of fine restaurants has made your mouth pucker for some really good California wine, check out the stores listed below for the two absolutely best collections of California wines in San Francisco (and probably the universe):

Draper and Esquin

Here you'll find the best selection of California wines in the City. The wines are scattered about the floor in no-nonsense crates, making it a bit difficult to comfortably browse. The clerks are knowledgeable and helpful, though, and can steer you to particularly good buys.

Draper and Esquin is at 655 Sutter Street, downtown. It's open Mon.-Fri., 10 a.m.-5:30 p.m., and Saturday 11 a.m.-4 p.m. Phone 885-4885.

Wine and Cheese Center

A more inviting store is the Wine and Cheese Center on Union Street.

Here you can even sit down to taste selected wines by the glass or buy your own bottle to cork and quaff on the premises.

The Wine and Cheese Center is at 2111 Union Street. They're open Mon.-Fri., 10 a.m.-7 p.m., and Saturday 11 a.m.-6 p.m. They offer wine tastings Wed.-Sat., noon till closing. Phone 563-3603.

100 Rent a Picnic

Still haven't left your heart in San Francisco? Unless you want to put out for another book, you'd better let this one get to you. Fortunately, it shouldn't be too hard.

Imagine a picnic. Any picnic, anywhere in San Francisco. Now call Little Red Riding Hood to have your picnic produced. Yup, not simply prepared, but produced. Klaus Lange, owner of Little Red Riding Hood, has catered picnics for up to 10,000 people at a time. He just loves a challenge. Give him a chance and he'll inject your picnic with as much style, wit and romance as your budget can stand. He'll arrange to have you taken up in a hot air balloon or set out to sea in a chartered yacht. He'll have you serenaded by a string quartet or charaded by a gaggle of mimes. In short, he'll stone woo you with flourishes such as a wicker basket, checkered tablecloth, Victorian bouquet—even a hot and sentimental love poem. If all this doesn't get you, see a cardiologist.

Little Red Riding Hood is at 885 Bush Street (at Taylor Street). Call a week ahead if you're going in for the bizarre, but at least three days in advance. Expect to spend at least $50 for a basket for two. Little Red Riding Hood will also provide you with a map to an appropriate picnic site, based on your mood and need for privacy. Phone 776-4555.

101 GET A LITTLE NO-FRILLS RELIGION

Church? But this is supposed to be a vacation.

Hold on—Glide Memorial is no ordinary church, thanks to the bombastic presence of Reverend Cecil Williams. (If the name has a familiar ring, it's because two of the SLA-Patty Hearst communiques were addressed to Williams.)

Twice a Sunday, Williams gathers up the human refuse around his Tenderloin District church, jumps out in front of their slow descent into hell and turns them into a miraculous parade of saints. If you don't think that's something, you ought to see him do it.

Cecil Williams holds his "Celebrations" (don't call them "Sermons") every Sunday at 9 a.m. and 11 a.m. Glide Memorial Church (it's Methodist, by the way) is at the corner of Ellis and Taylor, smack dab in the middle of the tough Tenderloin District, but just two blocks from Union Square. Phone 771-6300.

102 PSSST—WANTA HAVE A GOOD TIME FOR A NICKEL?

A classic piece of puffery out at San Francisco's historic Cliff House restaurant advises that "No Trip to San Francisco is Complete Until You've Seen the Mechanical Museum." Well, that's stretching it some, but if you do make it out to the Cliff House, you'll enjoy the unassuming collection of turn-of-the-century nickelodeons, mechanical wonders and penny arcade amusements that have been gathered in the Mechanical Museum. The unique collection was hauled over from the nearby Sutro Baths (see #41), which owner Adolph Sutro stocked with all manner of diversions in an attempt to draw customers. When the Sutro Baths closed, most of its contents were relocated.

The Mechanical Museum is in the lower level of the Cliff House, on the ocean. To get there, take Geary Avenue out of downtown and head for the ocean. You'll come on to the Cliff House just before you reach the ocean. The museum is free, but the amusements (all in working condition) do take your standard small change. Open seven days a week, 11 a.m. until at least 5 p.m. Phone 386-1170.

103 Get Out of Town

Has your San Francisco affair left you a little short of the return fare? No problem. If you use one of the ride services below, you'll save yourself the cost of this book and lunch money to boot.

Half Cost Car Pool Transit Systems. 2720 Grove Street, Berkeley. 845-1769. Open Mon.-Fri., 9 a.m.-6 p.m.

Despite the cumbersome title, this is easily the most efficient way to score a ride in the Bay Area. Half Cost is one person—Ralph—and he has but one aim: to get you out of town. He'll do it one of five ways: 1. Line you up with riders for your own car, each paying you half the gas (if you take two riders you break even, if you take three you make money). 2. Refer you to someone who needs a rider—you pay half their gas. 3. Refer you to a Driveaway agency. 4. Book you on one of the alternative buses. 5. Find you a rental car.

If you want to list a ride you can do so for free. If you need one, you'll have to buy Ralph's listing, which will entitle you or any friend to use his service for the next six months.

Haight Ashbury Switchboard. 387-7000. Open Mon.-Sun., 9 a.m.-10 p.m.

The ride service is only one of the many services offered by the Haight Ashbury Switchboard. They list you, if you have a ride to offer. If you need a ride, call them for a read-out. Free.

Underground Head Shop. 1588 Market Street. 864-5663. Open Mon.-Sun., noon-5 p.m.

You list if you have a ride or need one. The switchboard is a sideline activity, and while a gracious gesture to the community, it's not very complete. Free.

KTIM Ride Line. 100.9 FM. 456-1009. 1040 B Street, San Rafael, CA 94901.

The most fun of the ride lines. You call the station and list yourself right on the air. If you're shy, you can mail them the information and they'll read it for you. Free.

Alternative Buses

Grey Rabbit, Green Tortoise, American Gypsy, and Rainbow Express are four of the different (very) driver-owned, converted diesels that run between the two coasts and up and down the west coast. The trip from San Francisco to New York takes about three-and-one-half days, although you can get off anywhere in between for a proportionate amount of the full fare. Rather than deal with each of the lines separately, work through Half Cost Car Pool Transit Systems, listed above, or the Berkeley Ride Center, listed below.

Berkeley Ride Center. 524-5404. Open Mon.-Fri., 10 a.m.-5 p.m., Sat. 10 a.m.-1 p.m. (shorter hours in the winter)

They'll give you a read-out of rides and riders needed over the phone, as well as schedule you on one of the alternative bus lines. All you have to do is pick up your ticket at one of the outlets in San Francisco. Free.

Driveaways

If you qualify, Driveaways are a good way to go since you're traveling at your own pace and in your own space. Normally you have to be over twenty-one with a valid driver's license, leave a $100 cash deposit behind (refunded at the end of your trip) and provide a couple of local references. The Driveaway agency usually supplies the first tank of gas. Since the agencies tend to come and go, try classification 70 in the *Chronicle* want ads if these leads don't pan out:

AAA Automated Auto Transport. 589-1745. Millbrae (near the San Francisco airport). 9 a.m.-5 p.m.

Aaacon Auto Transport. 864-8800. 1095 Market Street. 9:30 a.m.-3:30 p.m.

Auto Driveaway Company. 777-3740. 785 Market Street. 9 a.m.-5 p.m.

104 Make Yourself Feel Right At Home

Alright, so maybe everybody's favorite city isn't your cup of tea at all. Maybe you like your streets flat and your men straight, your summers hot and your food not.

Face it—you're homesick. And if you still have two nights and three days left before you can get back to where you once belonged, you're stuck. Unless you consult the handy guide below, which will show you where to catch up on what's been going on back home, where to find a few reassuring friends, where to even find a familiar taste of home:

Out-of-town newspapers (some 84 in all, plus 36 foreign language papers): Harold's, 484 Geary Street

"Doonesbury": *San Francisco Chronicle*

NBC: Channel 4   **CBS:** Channel 5   **ABC:** Channel 7

Walter Cronkite: 7 p.m., Channel 5

"I Love Lucy": 6:30 p.m., Channel 2

"Rocky Horror Picture Show": Friday and Saturday at midnight at the Strand Theatre, 1127 Market Street.

Department Stores: Macy's, Stockton and O'Farrell Streets; Emporium, 835 Market Street.

Saks Fifth Avenue: Grant Avenue at Maiden Lane.

Brooks Brothers: 201 Post Street.

Sears: Geary Boulevard and Masonic Avenue.

Holiday Inn: Several locations, including Van Ness Avenue and Pine Street.

McDonald's: Various locations, including 609 Market Street.

Top 40: KFRC, AM 610

Middle-of-the-Road: KNBR, AM 680

Main Street: Market Street, between 4th and 8th Streets

Funky Broadway: Broadway, between Stockton and Montgomery Streets

FOOD AND BEER

Maine Lobster: Mainely Lobster, 2183 Greenwich Street

New England clam chowder: Salmagundi's, 442 Geary Street

Boston brown bread: Jurgensen's Grocery Company, 2190 Union Street

Egg cream soda, blackout cake and Zee's cheesecake (New York): New York City Deli, 2295 Market Street

Nathan's-style kosher hot dog (New York): Noble Frankfurter, 3159 Fillmore Street

Crab cakes (Baltimore): Better Value Foods, 1434 Connecticut Street

Hoagies (Philadelphia): Woolworth's, 898 Market Street

Ham hocks, greens and black-eyed peas (the South): Mozell's Kitchen, 808 Divisadero Street

Pecan pie (the South): Just Desserts, 1469 Pacific Avenue

Creole gumbo and New Orleans oyster loaf (New Orleans): Connie's Why Not Restaurant, 878 Valencia Street

Deep-dish pizza (Chicago): Harpo's, 2800 Leavenworth Street

Brautwurst (Milwaukee): Hofbrau, 219 O'Farrell Street

Swedish Meatballs (Minneapolis): Scandinavian Delicatessen, 2251 Market Street

Famous Amos Chocolate Chip cookies (Los Angeles): Macy's Gourmet Shop, Stockton and O'Farrell Streets

Maui Wowee Potato Chips (Hawaii): Jurgensen's Grocery Company, 2190 Union Street

Garden State Beer (New Jersey), **Porter Beer** (Pottsville, PN), **Iron City Beer** (Pittsburgh), and **Schell's Beer** (Minnesota): The Cannery Gourmet Shop and Wine Cellars, 2801 Leavenworth Street

Cold Springs Beer (Minnesota): GET Liquors, 11 Lakeshore Plaza

Lucky Lager (Washington): Coit Liquors, 585 Columbus Avenue

105 Fifty Famous San Franciscans' Favorite Restaurants

If there's one thing that a San Franciscan enjoys almost as much as eating out, it's talking about the experience. (And judging by the sheer number of restaurants in the City, San Franciscans *do* love eating out.) Why, you can hardly work up a good appetite in this town unless you can skillfully joust and parry about old-line restaurants and rejoin with a tantalizing turn-on or two. You haven't even begun to know San Francisco until you begin to know its restaurants. The task, delightfully, is delectable.

But where to begin. The number and variety of restaurants in San Francisco is staggering. A guide is in order, but most are of limited value, being the arbitrary opinion of one reviewer. Besides, the best way to hear about a restaurant is from a friend or trusted acquaintance. That way, you can align your own expectations with your trust in their taste.

Here then, is the better mousetrap: the actual restaurants where fifty real San Franciscans really eat when their own hunger and honor are on the line. You'll find nearly every imaginable food represented, from hot dog to haute cuisine. And you're sure to find a famous San Franciscan or two who's taste is as impeccable as your own. Bon appetite, and have a wonderful time in San Francisco.

Fifty Famous San Franciscans' Favorite Five

1. Mama's *Three locations. The original is at 1701 Stockton Street, 362-6421. American. Breakfast, lunch, dinner. Cash only.*

2. Washington Square Bar and Grill *1707 Powell Street, 982-8123. Continental. Lunch, dinner, Sunday brunch. All major credit cards.*

3. Vanessi's *498 Broadway, 421-0890. Northern Italian. Lunch, dinner. All major credit cards.*

4. Scoma's *Pier 47, Fisherman's Wharf, 771-4383. Seafood. Lunch, dinner. All major credit cards.*

5. Le Central *543 Bush Street, 391-2233. Bistro/French. Lunch, dinner. All major credit cards.*

Kurt Herbert Adler, *General Director, San Francisco Opera*

L'Orangerie *419 O'Farrell Street, 776-3600. French. Dinner. Dress code. Reservations required. All major credit cards.*

Joan Baez, *humanitarian*

Robert Restaurant Français *1701 Octavia Street, 931-1030. French. Dinner. All major credit cards.*

Le Club *1250 Jones Street, 771-5400. French. Dinner. Dress code. Reservations required. All major credit cards.*

Coffee Cantata *2030 Union Street, 931-0770. International. Lunch, dinner, Sunday brunch. All major credit cards.*

Marty Balin, *rock n roll outlaw*

Vanessi's *498 Broadway, 421-0890. Northern Italian. Lunch, dinner. All major credit cards.*

Pepper Mill *1850 Redwood Highway, Corte Madera, 924-1830. American. Breakfast, lunch, dinner. V, MC.*

El Paseo *7 El Paseo, Mill Valley, 388-0741. French Country. Dinner. Cash only.*

Rick Barry, *former Golden State Warrior*

La Bourgogne *330 Mason Street,*

362-7352. French. Dinner. Dress code. Reservations required. All major credit cards.

Lehr's Steak House *Taylor and Ellis Streets, 673-6800. Dinner. Reservations required. All major credit cards.*

Fior D'Italia *601 Union Street, 986-1886. Italian. Lunch, dinner. Reservations required. All major credit cards.*

Melvin Belli, *attorney*

Scoma's *Pier 47, 771-4383. Seafood. Lunch, dinner. All major credit cards.*

Tadich Grill *240 California Street, 391-2373. Seafood. Lunch, dinner. Cash only.*

Jack's *615 Sacramento Street, 986-9854. French. Lunch, dinner. Dress code. Reservations required. Cash only.*

Tony Bennett, *entertainer*

L'Etoile *1075 California Street, 771-1529. French. Dinner. Dress code. Reservations required. All major credit cards.*

Orsi's *375 Bush Street, 981-6535. Italian, continental. Lunch, dinner. All major credit cards.*

Fior D'Italia *601 Union Street, 986-1886. Italian. Lunch, dinner. Reservations required. All major credit cards.*

Vida Blue, *San Francisco Giant*

Ernie's *847 Montgomery Street, 397-5969. French. Dinner. Dress code. Reservations required. All major credit cards.*

Julius Castle *302 Greenwich Street, 362-3042. Continental. Lunch, dinner. Reservations required. All major credit cards.*

Wendy's Hamburgers *Beach and Leavenworth Streets and various locations.*

Tim Boxell, *artist extraordinaire*

Fournou's Ovens *905 California Street, 989-1910. Continental. Lunch, dinner. Dress code. Reservations required. All major credit cards.*

Hunan Restaurant *924 Sansome Street, 956-7727. Hunan. Lunch, dinner. All major credit cards.*

North Beach Restaurant *1512 Stockton Street, 392-1587. Italian. Lunch, dinner. Reservations recommended. All major credit cards.*

Willie Brown, *dapper politician*

Le Central *453 Bush Street, 391-2233. Bistro/French. Lunch, dinner. All major credit cards.*

Amelio's *1630 Powell Street, 397-4339. Northern Italian. Dinner. All major credit cards.*

Herb Caen, *columnist*

Trader Vic's *20 Cosmo Place,*

776-2232. Polynesian. Lunch, dinner. Dress code. Reservations recommended. All major credit cards.

L'Etoile *1075 California Street, 771-1529. French. Dinner. Dress code. Reservations required. All major credit cards.*

Le Central *543 Bush Street, 391-2233. Bistro/French. Lunch, dinner. Reservations required. V, MC.*

Delices de France *320 Mason Street, 433-7560. French. Breakfast, lunch, dinner. All major credit cards.*

Carol Doda, *entertainer*

Vanessi's *498 Broadway, 421-0890. Northern Italian. Lunch, dinner. All major credit cards.*

Cho-Cho *1020 Kearny Street, 397-3066. Japanese. Lunch, dinner. Reservations required. V, MC, DC.*

Mama's *1701 Stockton Street, 362-6421. American. Breakfast, lunch, dinner. Cash only.*

Doobie Brothers, *rock group:*

Jeff "Skunk" Baxter, *guitarist*

East West/Miyako Hotel *Post and Laguna Streets, 922-3200. Japanese/American. Breakfast, lunch, dinner. All major credit cards.*

Scoma's *Pier 47, 771-4383. Seafood. Lunch, dinner. All major credit cards.*

A Bit of Indonesia *211 Clement*

Street, 752-4042. *Indonesian. Dinner. V, MC.*

John Hartman, *percussion*

USA Cafe *431 Columbus Avenue, 731-4142. Home-style Italian. Breakfast, lunch. Cash only.*

Mama's *1701 Stockton Street, 362-6421. American. Breakfast, lunch, dinner. Cash only.*

Zim's *Beach and Hyde Streets plus various locations. American. Breakfast, lunch, dinner. Cash only.*

Keith Knudsen, *percussion*

Mama's *1701 Stockton Street, 362-6421. American. Breakfast, lunch, dinner. Cash only.*

Washington Square Bar and Grill *1707 Powell Street, 982-8123. Continental. Lunch, dinner, Sunday brunch. All major credit cards.*

Michael McDonald, *vocals and keyboards*

Mama's *1701 Stockton Street, 362-6421. American. Breakfast, lunch, dinner. Cash only.*

Fairmont Venetian Room *950 Mason Street, 772-5163. Continental. Dinner and show. Dress code. Reservations required. All major credit cards.*

Washington Square Bar and Grill *1707 Powell Street, 982-8123. Continental. Lunch, dinner, Sunday brunch. All major credit cards.*

Tiran Porter, *bass*

Mama's *1701 Stockton Street, 362-6421. American. Breakfast, lunch, dinner. Cash only.*

Washington Square Bar and Grill *1707 Powell Street, 982-8123. Continental. Lunch, dinner, Sunday brunch. All major credit cards.*

Joe Woo's *3011 Fillmore Street, 567-3066. Mandarin. Lunch, dinner. V, MC, DC.*

Pat Simmons, *guitarist*

Graziano's *453 Pine Street, 981-4800. Italian. Lunch.*

Joe Woo's *3011 Fillmore Street, 567-3066. Mandarin. Lunch, dinner. V, MC, DC.*

Mama's *1701 Stockton Street, 362-6421. American. Breakfast, lunch, dinner. Cash only.*

Margot Patterson Doss, *author*

Mingei Ya *2033 Union Street, 567-2553. Japanese. Dinner. All major credit cards.*

The Tandoori *2550 Van Ness Avenue, 776-1455. Indian. Breakfast, lunch, dinner. All major credit cards.*

Roosevelt Tamale Parlor *2817 24th Street, 648-9899. Mexican. Lunch, dinner. Cash only.*

Hugh Downs, *host of "Over Easy"*

Robert Restaurant Français *1701 Octavia Street, 931-1030. French.*

Dinner. V, MC, AE.

Mama's *1177 California Street, 928-1004. Continental. Breakfast, lunch, dinner. V.*

Johnny Kan's *708 Grant Avenue, 982-2388. Cantonese. Lunch, dinner. All major credit cards.*

Mimi Fariña, *entertainer and founder of Bread and Roses*

Henderson's *60 Corte Madera Avenue, Corte Madera, 924-8161. California cuisine. Lunch, dinner. Cash only.*

Robert Restaurant Français *1701 Octavia Street, 931-1030. French. Dinner. All major credit cards.*

Sanpei *1581 Webster Street, 922-2290. Japanese. Dinner. Cash only.*

Ben Fong-Torres, *journalist*

Le Central *453 Bush Street, 391-2233. Bistro/French. Lunch, dinner. Reservations required. V, MC.*

The Hungry Mouth *9 Clement Street, 221-8403. Natural Foods. Breakfast, lunch, dinner. V, MC.*

Lou Galliani, *close friend and San Francisco intimate*

Saigon Restaurant *579 Geary Street, 885-3332. Vietnamese. Lunch, dinner. V, MC.*

Luisa's Ristorante Italiano *1509 Polk Street, 771-6363. Italian. Lunch, dinner. V, MC.*

Carlene's of Maui *1237 Polk Street, 441-8200. Breakfast, lunch, dinner, Sunday brunch. V, DC.*

Herbert Gold, *novelist*

Washington Square Bar and Grill *1707 Powell Street, 982-8123. Continental. Lunch, dinner, Sunday brunch. All major credit cards.*

Pipat's *500 Broadway, 982-9934. French and Thai. Lunch, dinner. All major credit cards.*

Jalisco Cafe *2487 Mission Street, 285-2653. Mexican. Lunch, dinner. Cash only.*

Bill Graham, *rock impresario*

Vanessi's *498 Broadway, 421-0890. Northern Italian. Lunch, dinner. All major credit cards.*

El Paseo *7 El Paseo, Mill Valley, 388-0741. French country. Dinner. Cash only.*

Guernica's *2009 Bridgeway, Sausalito, 332-1512. French Basque. Dinner. All major credit cards.*

Dashiell Hammett, *author*

Jack's *615 Sacramento Street, 986-9854. French. Lunch, dinner. Dress code. Reservation required. Cash only.*

Jay Hansen, *yours truly*

Original Joe's *144 Taylor Street,
775-4877. Italian. Lunch, dinner.
Cash only.*
La Pantera Cafe *1234 Grant Avenue,
392-0170. Italian home style. Lunch,
dinner. Cash only.*
Yen Ching *939 Kearny, 397-3543.
Hunan, Szechwan. Lunch, dinner.
All major credit cards.*

Dan Hicks, *entertainer*

Clown Alley *2442 Columbus Avenue
and various locations. Hamburgers,
hot dogs, fries.*
Garden Court at the Sheraton Palace
*Market at New Montgomery Streets,
392-8600. Continental. Breakfast,
lunch, Sunday brunch. Reservations
required for brunch. All major credit
cards.*
A Sabella's *Jefferson and Taylor
Streets, 771-6775. Seafood. Lunch,
dinner. Cash only.*

Jefferson Starship, *rock group:*

David Freiberg, *keyboards*

Otafuku Tei *1737 Buchanan Street,
931-1578. Japanese. Lunch, dinner.
Cash only.*

Paul Kantner, *guitarist*

Vanessi's *498 Broadway, 421-0890.
Northern Italian. Lunch, dinner. All
major credit cards.*

The Vintner *1875 Union Street,
922-4498. Continental. Lunch, dinner, Sunday brunch. All major credit
cards.*
Enrico's *504 Broadway, 392-6220.
Continental. Lunch, dinner. All major
credit cards.*

Pete Sears, *bass*

Shizuya *45 Caledonia Street, Sausalito, 332-2013. Japanese. Dinner.
V, MC.*
Taj of India *825 Pacific Avenue,
392-0089. Indian. Dinner. All major
credit cards.*
464 Magnolia *464 Magnolia, Larkspur, 924-6831. Continental. Lunch,
dinner, Sunday brunch. V, MC, AE.*

Grace Slick, *vocals*

Doggie Diner *601 Van Ness Avenue
and various locations. Hamburgers,
hot dogs, fries.*

Journey, *rock group (consensus)*

Julius Castle *302 Greenwich Street,
362-3042. Continental. Lunch, dinner. Reservations required. All major
credit cards.*
Swan Oyster Bar *1517 Polk Street,
673-1101. Seafood. Lunch. Cash
only.*
El Faro *2399 Folsom Street,
647-3716. Mexican. Breakfast,
lunch. Cash only.*

Paul Krassner, *perpetrator of* The Realist

Dipti Nivas *216 Church Street, 626-6411. Vegetarian. Lunch, dinner. Cash only.*

Oasis Juice Bar *Natural food. 449 Castro Street, 863-0735. Lunch, dinner. Cash only.*

Cafe Strand *288 Noe Street, 864-9667. Mediterranean. Breakfast, lunch, dinner. Cash only.*

Jim Lange, *"Dating Game" host*

Modesto Lanzone's *900 North Point Street, 771-2880. Northern Italian. Lunch, dinner. Reservations required. All major credit cards.*

Grison's *2100 Van Ness Avenue, 673-1888. Steak. Dinner. All major credit cards.*

Le Club *1250 Jones Street, 771-5400. French. Dinner. Dress code. Reservations required. All major credit cards.*

Cyril Magnin, *Mr. San Francisco*

Ciao *230 Jackson Street, 982-9500. Italian. Lunch, dinner. Reservations required. All major credit cards.*

MacArthur Park *607 Front Street, 398-5700. American. Lunch, dinner, Sunday brunch. Reservations recommended. All major credit cards.*

Imperial Palace *919 Grant Avenue, 982-4440. Cantonese. Lunch, din-*

ner. *Dress code. All major credit cards.*

Karl Malden, *actor*

L'Etoile *1075 California Street, 771-1529. French. Dinner. Dress code. Reservations required. All major credit cards.*

Tadich Grill *240 California Street, 391-2373. Seafood. Lunch, dinner. Cash only.*

Mama's *1177 California Street, 928-1004. Continental. Breakfast, lunch, dinner. V.*

Armistead Maupin, *author of* Tales of the City

Washington Square Bar and Grill *1707 Powell Street, 982-8123. Continental. Lunch, dinner, Sunday brunch. All major credit cards.*

L'Orangerie *419 O'Farrell Street, 776-3600. French. Dinner. Dress code. Reservations required. All major credit cards.*

Dipti Nivas *216 Church Street, 626-6411. Vegetarian. Lunch, dinner. Cash only.*

Willie McCovey, *legend*

Scoma's *Pier 47, 771-4383. Seafood. Lunch, dinner. All major credit cards.*

Ernie's *847 Montgomery Street, 397-5969. French. Dinner. Dress* code. *Reservations required. All major credit cards.*

Monroe's *1968 Lombard Street, 567-4550. French/Continental. Dinner. Reservations required. V, MC, AE.*

Cyra McFadden, *author of* The Serial

Morty's *1979 Union Street, 922-6133. Italian. Lunch, dinner, Sunday brunch. V, MC.*

El Paseo *7 El Paseo, Mill Valley, 388-0741. French country. Dinner. Cash only.*

Saigon Restaurant *579 Geary Street, 885-3332. Vietnamese. Lunch, dinner. V, MC.*

Alejandro's *1840 Clement Street, 668-1184. Spanish and Mexican. Dinner. V, MC.*

Liz Metzger, *author of* The Breakfast Book, *a guide to Bay Area breakfast spots*

Cafe Lido *373 Broadway, 391-7524. Continental. Breakfast, lunch, Sunday brunch. All major credit cards.*

Doidge's Kitchen *2217 Union Street, 921-2149. American. Breakfast, lunch. All major credit cards.*

Duboce Lunch *1700 Mission Street, 863-4177. Breakfast, lunch. Cash only.*

Jim Mitchell, *filmmaker*

May's Cafe *955 Larkin Street,* *474-5276. Cantonese/American. Lunch, dinner. Cash only.*

Asian Queen *730 Larkin Street, 474-6681. Chinese. Lunch, dinner. Cash only.*

Pablo Cruise, *rock group (consensus)*

Trident *558 Bridgeway, Sausalito, 332-1334. Natural foods. Lunch, dinner. V, MC.*

Scoma's *Pier 47, 771-4383. Seafood. Lunch, dinner. All major credit cards.*

Carlos Santana, *guitarist*

Dipta Nivas *216 Church Street, 626-6411. Vegetarian. Lunch, dinner. Cash only.*

Gaylord's *Ghirardelli Square, 771-8822. Indian. Lunch, dinner. All major credit cards.*

Mama's *1701 Stockton Street, 362-6421. American. Breakfast, lunch, dinner. Cash only.*

Boz Scaggs, *entertainer*

Perry's *1944 Union Street, 922-9022. American. Breakfast, lunch, dinner. V, AE.*

John's Grill *63 Ellis Street, 986-0069. Continental. Lunch, dinner. V, MC.*

Le Central *453 Bush Street, 391-2233. Bistro/French. Lunch, dinner. Reservations required. V, MC.*

Sam Spade, *private dick*

John's Grill   *63 Ellis Street, 986-0069. Continental. Lunch, dinner. V, MC.*

Sally Stanford, *entrepreneur*

Sally Stanford's Valhalla Inn   *201 Bridgeway, Sausalito, 332-1792. Seafood. Lunch, dinner, Sunday brunch. All major credit cards.*
Ondine's   *558 Bridgeway, Sausalito, 332-0791. French/Continental. Dinner. Dress code. All major credit cards.*
Shizuya   *45 Caledonia Street, Sausalito, 332-2013. Japanese. Dinner. V, MC.*

Margo St. James, *private investigator*

Washington Square Bar and Grill   *1707 Powell Street, 982-8123. Italian/Continental. Lunch, dinner, Sunday brunch. All major credit cards.*
Hamburger Mary's   *1582 Folsom Street, 626-5767. Organic grill. Breakfast, lunch, dinner. V, MC.*
La Veranda   *1499 Grant Avenue, 397-8831. Italian. Lunch, dinner. Cash only.*

Lyle Tuttle, *tattooist*

Sai Yon   *641 Jackson Street, 989-3814.*
Original Joe's   *144 Taylor Street, 775-4877. Italian. Lunch, dinner. Cash only.*

Hamburger Mary's   *1582 Folsom Street, 626-5767. Organic grill. Breakfast, lunch, dinner. V, MC.*

Virginia Wade, *former Golden Gater tennis star*

La Pergola   *2060 Chestnut Street, 563-4500. Northern Italian. Dinner. Dress code. Reservations required. All major credit cards.*
Washington Square Bar and Grill   *1707 Powell Street, 982-8123. Italian/Continental. Lunch, dinner, Sunday brunch. All major credit cards.*

Gene Washington, *former San Francisco 49er*

Le Club   *1250 Jones Street, 771-5400. French/Continental. Dinner. Dress code. Reservations required. All major credit cards.*
Imperial Palace   *919 Grant Avenue, 982-4440. Cantonese. Lunch, dinner. Dress code. All major credit cards.*

Cecil Williams, *community activist*

Toro-ya   *1734 Post Street, 931-5200. Japanese. Lunch, dinner. Cash only.*
Robert Restaurant Francais   *1701 Octavia Street, 931-1030. French. Dinner. All major credit cards.*
The Waterfront   *Pier 7, 391-2696. Seafood. Lunch, dinner, Sunday brunch. Reservations required. All major credit cards.*

Index

Thanks, Myra